SUNDAY GOSPEL

doodle notebook

doodle notes™
learning benefits of visual note-taking

stronger **focus**

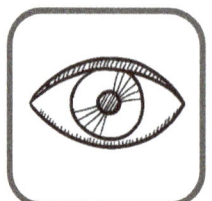
retention through dual coding

mental connections

memory **boost**

communication between **brain** hemispheres

building long-term memories

activated **neural** pathways

increased **creativity** & alertness

associative recognition

picture superiority **effect**

relaxation **benefits**

problem solving skills boost

The Gospel Doodle Note Book lets students use creativity to learn more about each Sunday Gospel and reflect on it.

As they color, doodle, and pray their way through the year's Gospels, students will explore both factual information and personal applications of the Gospel message in their own lives.

This book is perfect for a Sunday School Faith Formation class, a Catholic school, homeschool, or even just for personal use.

Terms of Use

Thanks so much for purchasing this book!

This resource is licensed to be used by a single student only.

All rights reserved.

Copying pages is prohibited.

For a PDF ebook version that you can print and copy, you can purchase a teacher license at gospeldoodlenotes.com

© Copyright 2024
Catechetical Chameleon

Clip Art & Font Credit

Sunday Gospel doodle notes

doodle notebook

What's Included?

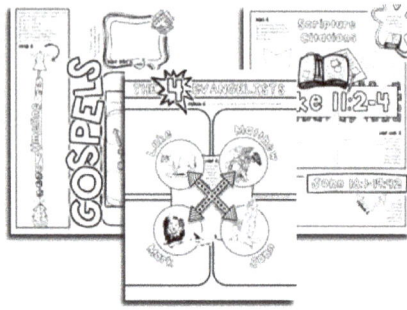

Introductory Pages
to set the stage & learn about the Gospels, meet the Evangelists, and review how to read Scripture citations

Liturgical Seasons Cover Pages
Just for fun & organization!
(Students can color if they want to)

doodle notes®

What's Included?

Sample pages:

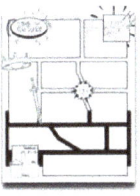  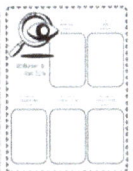    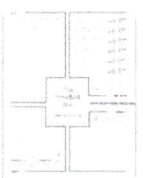 
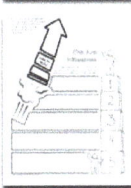 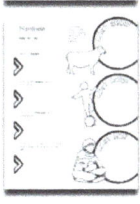 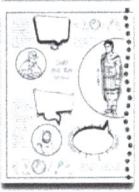 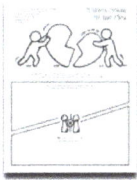   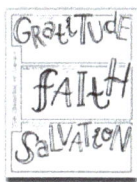 

Visual, Interactive "Doodle Note" Pages for Every Sunday Gospel
Students will doodle, color-code, sketch, reflect, color, think, and pray their way through the Gospels all year long

---

doodle notes®

What's Included?

A Blend of Factual Information and Guided Reflections

The student pages cover the details and background information, but they also provide connections to daily life and opportunities for reflection and prayer.

Teacher Guides

to provide background info and reflection & discussion questions

How to Use

Book Setup & Organization

The book is organized by liturgical season to make it easy to find each week's Gospel page, even as the liturgical calendar changes each year. This book is designed to be used with Cycle Year C, and will always work during years that follow Cycle C (every third year).

However, there will still be slight variations in the sequence of days. For example, if a Holy Day of Obligation happens to fall on a Sunday in a given year, then you may not use that particular Ordinary Time Gospel, since it is replaced with the one for that Holy Day instead.

So don't worry if you do not use a page during one year, and be aware that you will have to flip back and forth between sections in this book as you go through the seasons. For example, at one point in Ordinary Time, Lent begins and you will pause that section, flip ahead to Lent and Easter, and then go back to Ordinary Time once Easter is over.

Use the Table of Contents as a reference, and if you need additional support as you follow the liturgical calendar, the USCCB.org website is very helpful.

Bonus Pages

On the rare occasion that the Gospel that is read at mass for the week does not have a page in this book (like when a special holy day falls on a Sunday or another circumstance makes the calendar not match with any standard Gospel included here), you can use one of the bonus pages included in the back of the book. These additional doodle notes will offer your students a lesson for that day so they can still enjoy doing their doodle notes for the week. Enjoy!

While creating this book, I have prayed for you and your students who will use these pages. I hope that it works well for you and brings you and your kids closer to God as you walk through the Gospels together. I've gotten help from my wonderful team of family and friends including a priest, a seminarian, a Theology Department Head, and Catholic school teachers, all with expertise in Catholic theology. We've worked hard to make it as accurate and as helpful as possible. We've been praying for guidance as we form this content, and have also prayed for all of you who will use it. We hope you enjoy these reflections and grow spiritually from them. God bless you and your students!

How to Use

Teaching with Doodle Note Pages

Before using each page, read the Gospel passage aloud together. The Scripture citation is included on every single page to make this easy! Even if students have just heard it at mass, it is usually necessary to re-read it and have a printed copy available for them to access as a reference while they work through the pages. They can check the text as they answer questions, color, doodle, sketch, and add creative embellishments.

A wonderful website for the text of the Gospels is USCCB.org, and the version shown there is what these pages were directly based upon. However, your class set of Bibles or home Bible will do the trick too if you prefer that option.

One of the best ways to use the doodle note method is to do a teacher model. The easiest way to do this is to project/display a blank copy of the same doodle page that students have in front of them. Then, complete your "teacher copy" as you give notes. You can expand past it and add more notes on the board, talk through the lesson, and lecture as you normally would.

Even if you keep your note page "bare bones" and just fill in the blanks, your main job is to talk and model the concept and examples, just as you normally would. Students will have plenty of time to embellish their pages while you talk about the Gospel and explain more. They can also discuss it in small groups.

It can also be helpful to show completed samples to help inspire your students, at least the first few days until they get comfortable with the artistic aspect. You can save your own colored samples as you go, or collect a few student samples from previous years if you'd like. We've included a couple samples here and there to get you and your students inspired.

We recommend that you review **all** the directions on a page with the students before they begin. Sometimes they have to write or draw things in specific places. The goal is to help connect the visuals to the words in a way that helps them reflect, learn, and remember.

In any extra time, encourage students to include additional relevant doodles in the margins based on parts of the Scripture that strike them, or copy a line in creative lettering if it's something that they want to remember or pray about later.

How to Use

Teaching with Doodle Note Pages

Encourage creativity!

These pages are extremely flexible, and the best way to use them really depends on your own students and your classroom culture. Using the same page can go completely differently in your 1st period class than in your 2nd period class. Some classes will take it and run with it, and some will walk through it right alongside you as you fill it in together like a whole class graphic organizer.

There are really no "right ways" or "wrong ways" to teach with doodle notes. Be flexible, and if you would like more tips about this teaching strategy, I've got plenty of resources to help you along the way at doodlenotes.org

How to Use

Getting Started

The new Liturgical Calendar Year always begins with Advent.

The ideal time to begin this book is in the fall.

You can start with the introductory pages and cover one page per week in the three weeks **before** Advent begins if you wish. If you have more time in the fall, you can also use the Liturgical Calendar page in the "Bonus" section to review the seasons of the church year.

Then, throughout Advent, after each Sunday gospel, cover one page per week. Continue in a similar way from there on, using the book throughout the entire church year. You can use the pages each Monday if you are in a traditional classroom setting (or each Friday if you prefer to do it before the weekend Gospel and wind down for the end of the week). In a Sunday School Faith Formation class, or in a home setting, you can do these immediately after hearing the Sunday Gospel at mass.

If you are not starting in the fall, don't worry – you can just pick up wherever you are in the year. In this case, we do recommend that you go back and revisit the other pages in any free time, though. There are such wonderful lessons and reflection opportunities that can come from each different Gospel message, even if you are reading one that does not happen to correspond to the mass readings on any given day.

These visual interactive note pages offer a wonderful and relaxing way to connect with God in your own creative way as you reflect on His word. Any time that feels appropriate for a calm moment with Jesus is a great time to pull out the doodle notes.

A Reminder

You may have never thought about it, but **creativity** is one of God's greatest gifts to us. When we get creative, we're using something that we have in common with God, the creator of the universe!

How amazing is it that God, who created the entire world, decided to give us each our own creativity so that we can share in one of His own greatest joys! He generously shares with us the ability to produce something beautiful!

Pass this on to your students as you invite them to use their own creativity to worship and build their own relationship with the Creator through this book. As a bonus, creating something new is also great for mental health. So, get creative!

doodle notebook

contents

Cycle Year "C"

Pages are organized by liturgical season, so you will have to flip back and forth according to the transitions between Ordinary Time and Lent, for example, since the order of the Gospels will depend on the dates for the year. Similarly, additional Holy Days of Obligation are included in their own section even though they occur throughout the calendar year because the sequence of the Gospels will vary from year to year. The USCCB website has links to the updated liturgical calendar for any given year that you can reference as needed.

Use the teacher guide that corresponds to each visual doodle note reflection page to help you lead your students through the content.

	Student Page	Teacher Guide
Introduction		
- Gospels: The Good News	14	100 (Sample: 101)
- The 4 Evangelists	15	100 (Sample: 102)
- Scripture Citations	16	103
Advent		
- First Sunday of Advent	18	106
- Second Sunday of Advent	19	106
- Third Sunday of Advent	20	107 (Sample: 108)
- Fourth Sunday of Advent	21	107
Christmas		
- Christmas Vigil	24	110 (Sample: 111)
- Nativity of the Lord / Christmas Day	25	110
- The Holy Family	26	112
- Epiphany of the Lord	27	112

contents

Ordinary Time

	Student Page	Teacher Guide
Baptism of the Lord (1ˢᵗ Sunday of O.T.)	30	114-115 (Sample: 116)
Second Sunday of Ordinary Time	31	114
Third Sunday of Ordinary Time	32	117
Fourth Sunday of Ordinary Time	33	117
Fifth Sunday of Ordinary Time	34	118
Sixth Sunday of Ordinary Time	35	118 (Sample: 119)
Seventh Sunday of Ordinary Time	36	120
Eighth Sunday of Ordinary Time	37	120
Ninth Sunday of Ordinary Time	38	121
Tenth Sunday of Ordinary Time	39	121
Eleventh Sunday of Ordinary Time	40	122
Twelfth Sunday of Ordinary Time	41	122
Thirteenth Sunday of Ordinary Time	42	123
Fourteenth Sunday of Ordinary Time	43	123
Fifteenth Sunday of Ordinary Time	44	124
Sixteenth Sunday of Ordinary time	45	124
Seventeenth Sunday of Ordinary Time	46	125 (Sample: 126)
Eighteenth Sunday of Ordinary Time	47	125
Nineteenth Sunday of Ordinary Time	48	127
Twentieth Sunday of Ordinary Time	49	127
Twenty-First Sunday of Ordinary Time	50	128
Twenty-Second Sunday of Ordinary Time	51	128
Twenty-Third Sunday of Ordinary Time	52	129
Twenty-Fourth Sunday of Ordinary Time	53	129
Twenty-Fifth Sunday of Ordinary Time	54	130
Twenty-Sixth Sunday of Ordinary Time	55	130
Twenty-Seventh Sunday of Ordinary Time	56	131
Twenty-Eighth Sunday of Ordinary Time	57	131
Twenty-Ninth Sunday of Ordinary Time	58	132
Thirtieth Sunday of Ordinary Time	59	132
Thirty-First Sunday of Ordinary Time	60	133
Thirty-Second Sunday of Ordinary Time	61	133
Thirty-Third Sunday of Ordinary Time	62	134
Our Lord Jesus Christ, King of the Universe	63	134

contents

	Student Page	Teacher Guide
Lent		
- Ash Wednesday	66	136 (Sample: 137)
- First Sunday of Lent	67	136
- Second Sunday of Lent	68	138
- Third Sunday of Lent	69	138
- Fourth Sunday of Lent	70	139
- Fifth Sunday of Lent	71	139
- Palm Sunday	72	140 (Sample: 141)
- Holy Thursday	73	140
- Good Friday	74	142
Easter		
- Easter Sunday	76	144 (Sample: 145)
- Divine Mercy Sunday	77	144
- Third Sunday of Easter	78	146
- Fourth Sunday of Easter	79	146
- Fifth Sunday of Easter	80	147
- Sixth Sunday of Easter	81	148
- Seventh Sunday of Easter	82	149
- Ascension of the Lord	83	149
- Pentecost	84	150 (Sample: 151)
Additional Holy Days		
- Immaculate Conception	86	154
- Mary the Mother of God	87	154
- Feast of the Assumption	88	155
- All Saints Day	89	155 (Sample: 156)
Bonus Pages		
- The Armor of God	92-93	158-159
- The Liturgical Calendar	94	160-161
- Holy Week	95	162-163
Footnotes		164

INTRO TO THE GOSPELS

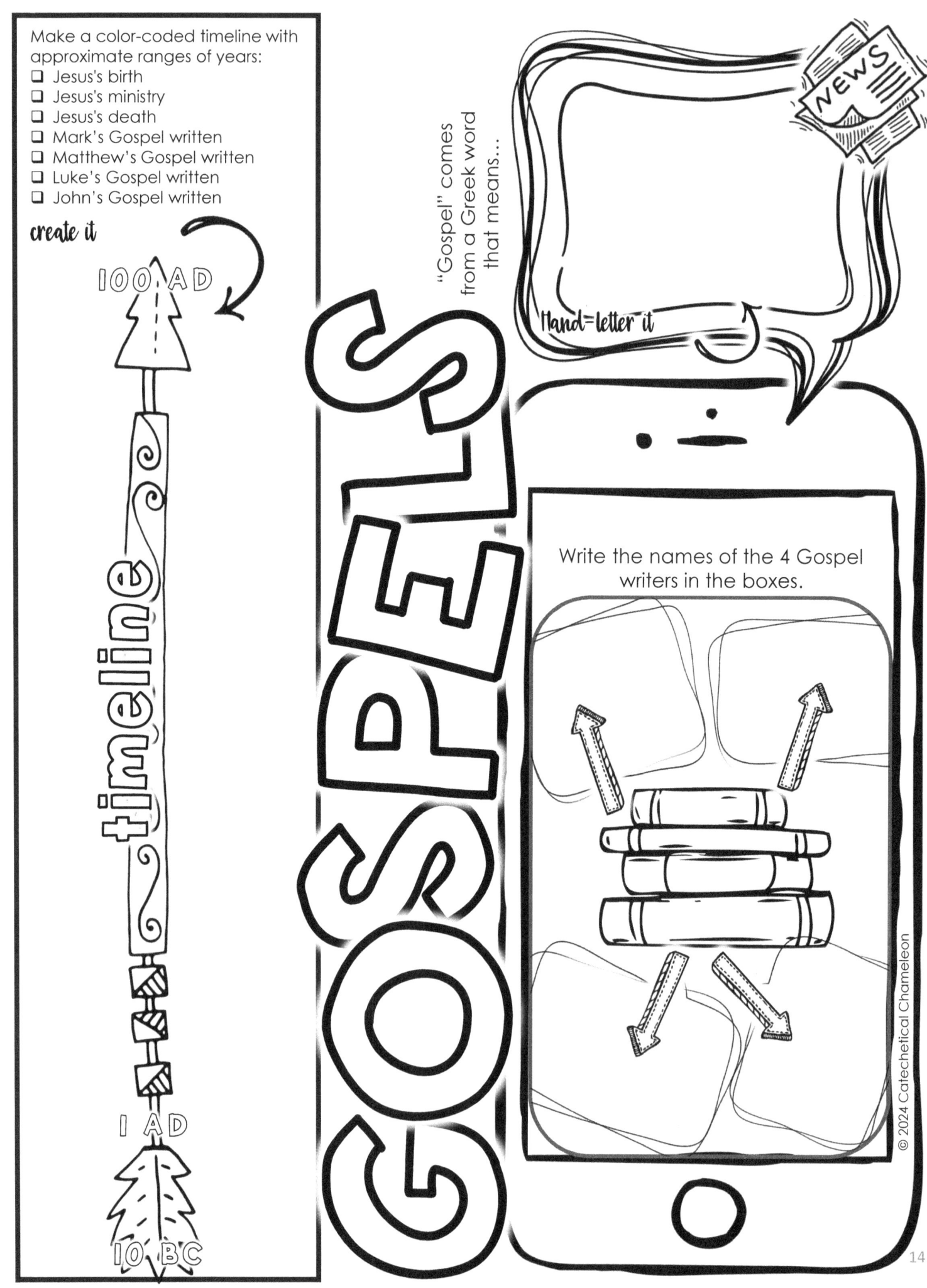

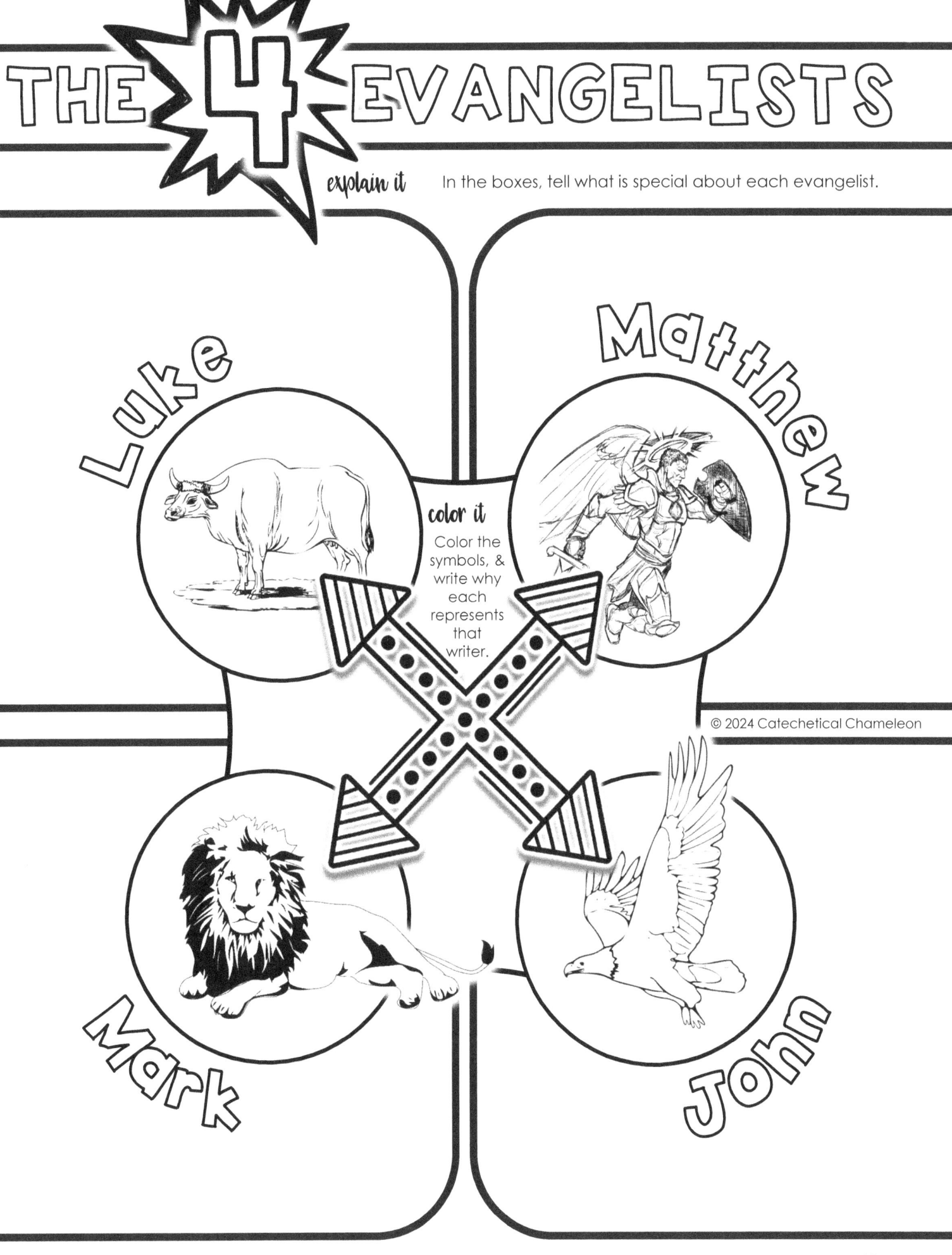

Scripture Citations

label it
In the arrows, identify:
- ☐ Verse (starting line #)
- ☐ Verse (stopping line #)
- ☐ Book
- ☐ Chapter

Remember, the Bible is a collection of many _____.

Luke 11:2-4

try it
Find this passage. What is this part of Luke's Gospel about?

Color code it
Use one color for the *book* and its arrow label, another for the *chapter*, and another for the *verses*.

© 2024 Catechetical Chameleon

try it
Find this passage. What is this part of John's Gospel about?

John 18:1-19:42

explain it

(This passage continues into another chapter. Explain how to read this.)

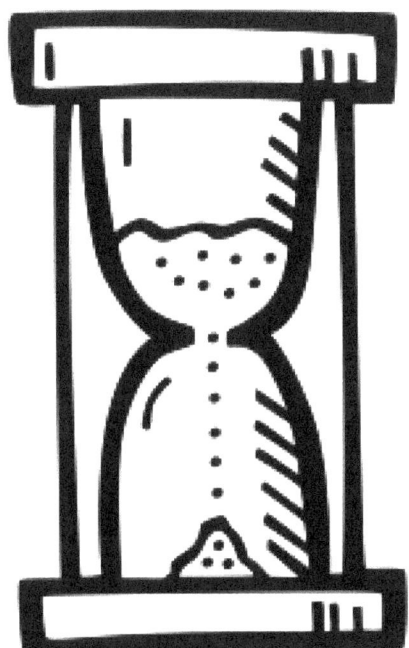

ADVENT

Make Straight His Paths

Sketch it
- Draw a hiker beneath the hat, holding the map and compass. (A stick figure is fine.)
- Sketch a dotted line showing a very long and winding trail that passes up and over, and all around the mountains.
- Next, *make straight his path* by adding tunnels and/or bridges to make a straight and level trail instead.

Luke 3:1-6

Reflect on it

What does this mean? How can we "prepare the way" for the Lord?

Explain it

What is the difference once you make the pathway straight and level?

Color it

Filled with Expectation

Luke 3:10-18

baptism with water

Compare the two. What is the cleansing power of water vs. the purifying property of fire? What does water represent? What does fire represent? Explain (both literally and spiritually) to tell what this means in this Gospel.

baptism with fire

To separate good produce from waste, a farmer would sort the good from the bad with a winnowing fan. It was a tool that was a cross between a fork and a shovel. By using it to toss the wheat into the air, the farmer could separate the wheat from the chaff. The kernels of wheat (good) would fall to the ground to gather. The lighter chaff (bad/waste) would be blown by the wind and then collected and burned up. Reflect on the meaning of this Gospel, and find the deeper meaning of what John says the Messiah will do. Then write and say a prayer asking for God's help based on your realizations.

Find the meaning:

Write a prayer:

The Visitation of Mary

Luke 1:39-45

Mary has faith in God's promises. Which of God's promises do you need to believe in more strongly than you do now?

Mary and Elizabeth have a friendship centered around their strong faith in God and their belief in His promises. How can you build friendships like this?

Label the people from this Gospel.

Quote a favorite line from Elizabeth in this Gospel and use creative lettering to write it.

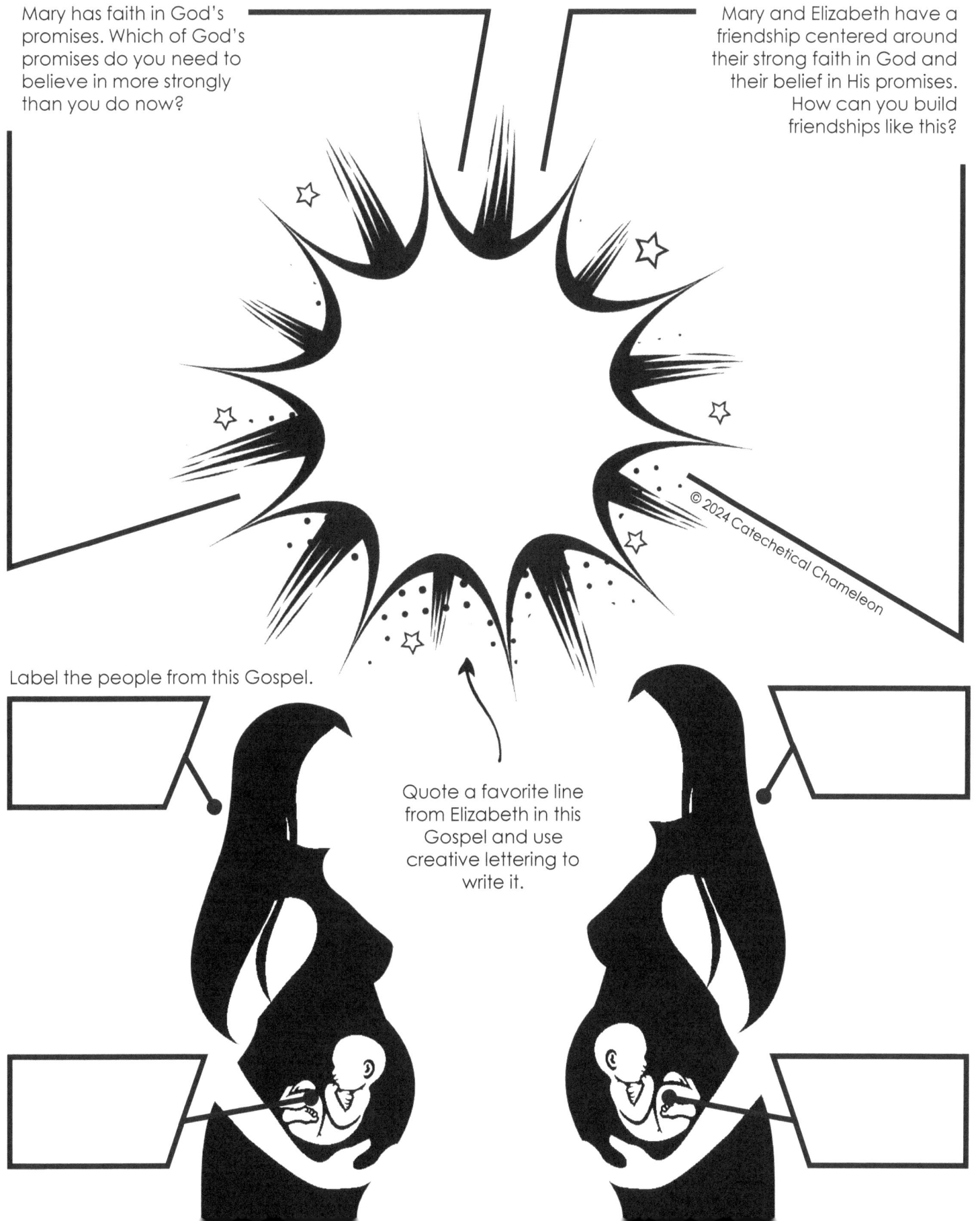

© 2024 Catechetical Chameleon

CHRISTMAS

How does the birth of Jesus fulfill God's promise to His people?

Why do you think that Matthew felt it was so important to track and document the full list of Jesus's ancestors? What does this list show us?

Somewhere in the image below, use creative lettering to sketch out a key word, phrase, or quote of your choice from this Gospel.

The Birth of Jesus

What is most surprising to you about the way that God sent Jesus into the world? Inside the boxes, use sketches or creative lettering to give 3 details about Jesus's birth that are unexpected. Then color as you reflect on the bigger picture. What is most incredible about God's plan here?

Matthew 1:1-25

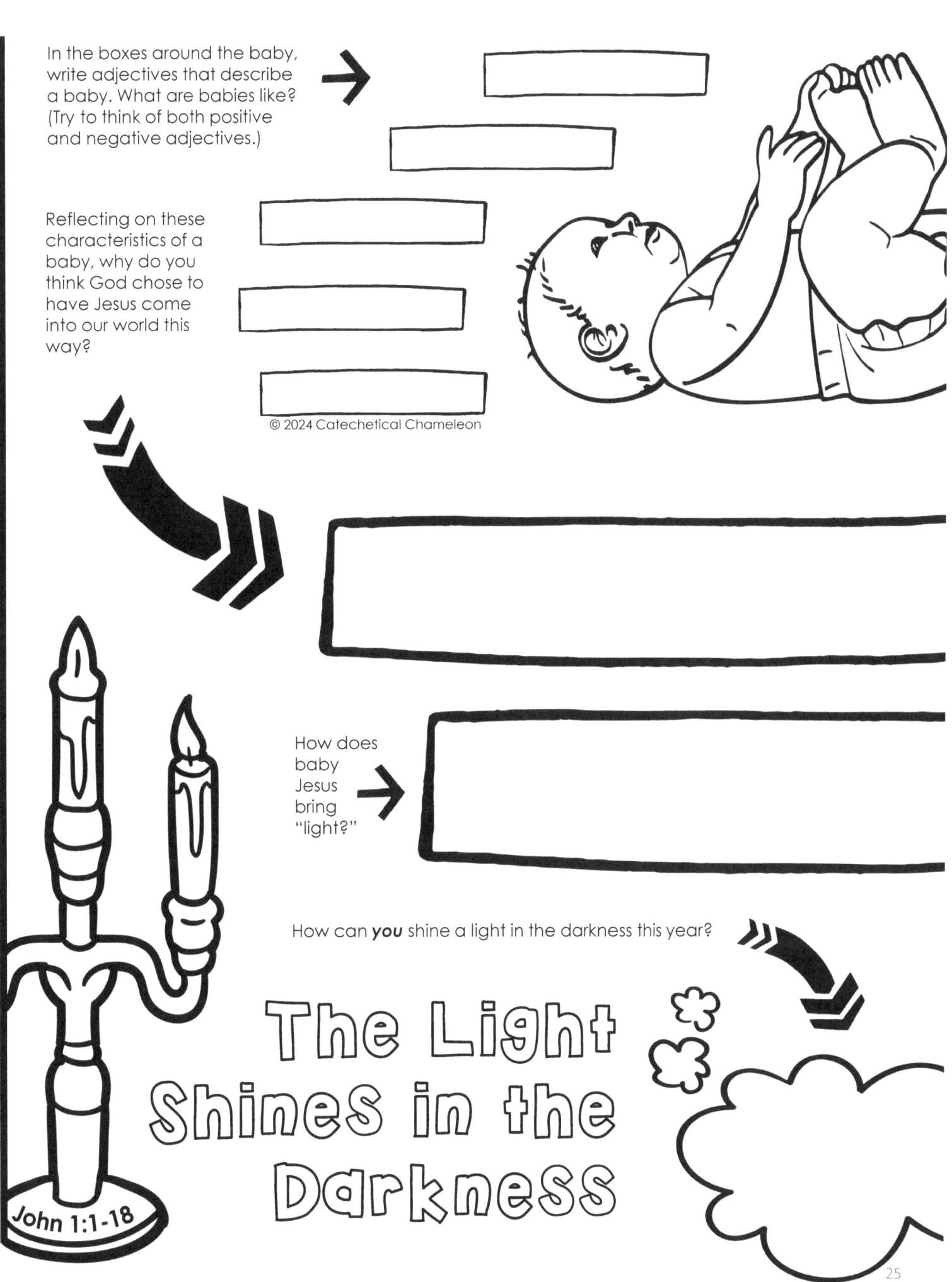

ORDINARY TIME

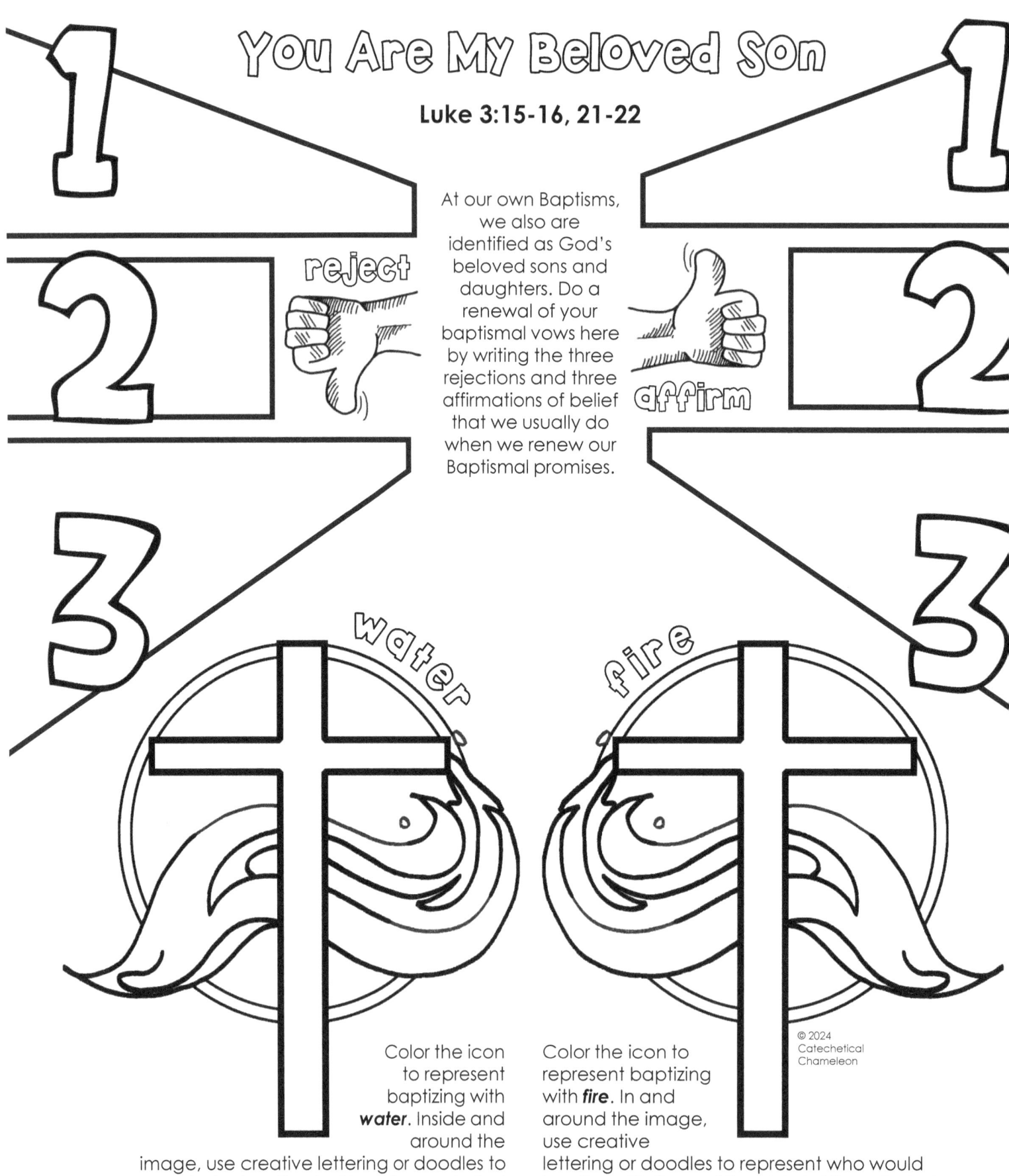

reflect on it
How would you feel if you returned to your home, and the people there rejected you and wanted to throw you off of a hill?

sketch it
Draw the final events (verses 28-30) in this Gospel above.

quote it
Find and copy Jesus's words for each below:

- telling the people that He was here to fulfill scripture through the Spirit of the Lord

- predicting the words of the people asking Him to perform miracles

- explaining in one simple sentence why those in Nazareth could not see Him as anything other than a simple carpenter's son

© 2024 Catechetical Chameleon

Jesus in Nazareth
Luke 4:21-30

Luke 5:1-11

Do Not Be Afraid

doodle it

This Gospel shows that Jesus did not just have wisdom as a teacher. He also showed that He had real, tangible, practical assistance to provide for the apostles in their daily work. Clearly He had the power of God behind Him! What in your own life would feel like this great "catch" and amaze you in the way that the catch of fish astonished the apostles? Have you talked to Jesus about it? Color the image while reflecting on this, and briefly jot some words about this inside the fish as you pray about it. Add creative doodles at the top of the page.

write it

What does it mean to be "catching men" from now on in this Gospel?

color it

pray about it

Why does Jesus have to tell them not to be afraid? What could be scary about dropping everything to follow Jesus? On the left, sketch two icons or images that represent things that the apostles may have risked losing in order to say yes to this call. On the right, sketch two icons or images that represent things *you* may have to be willing to risk losing if you say yes to Jesus's call in your own life.

sketch it

apostles

yourself

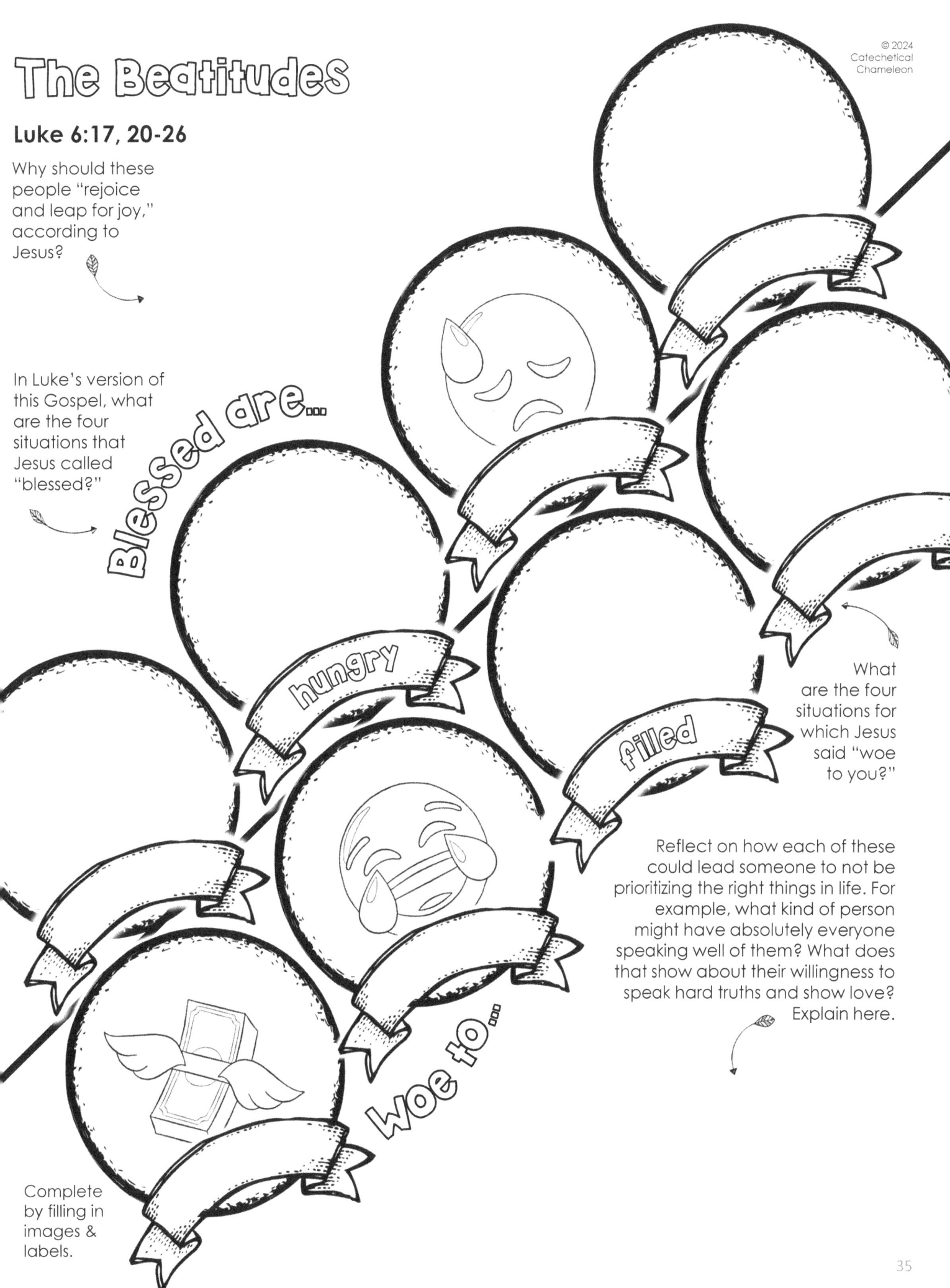

Be Merciful
Luke 6:27-38

do to others as you would have them do to you

Below, sketch 3 specific examples of how Jesus tells us to do this in this Gospel below. Then add a 4th of your own.

Take a moment to put this in action. Pray for someone who has mistreated you.

for the measure with which you measure will in return be measured out to you.

What kind of "measuring cup" do you want God to use when He judges you? Is that the same measuring cup that you are using when you think of others? In the measuring cup, use creative lettering to write some words about how you hope God will measure your goodness as well as your sins. Then reflect on whether you are measuring and judging others in the same way.

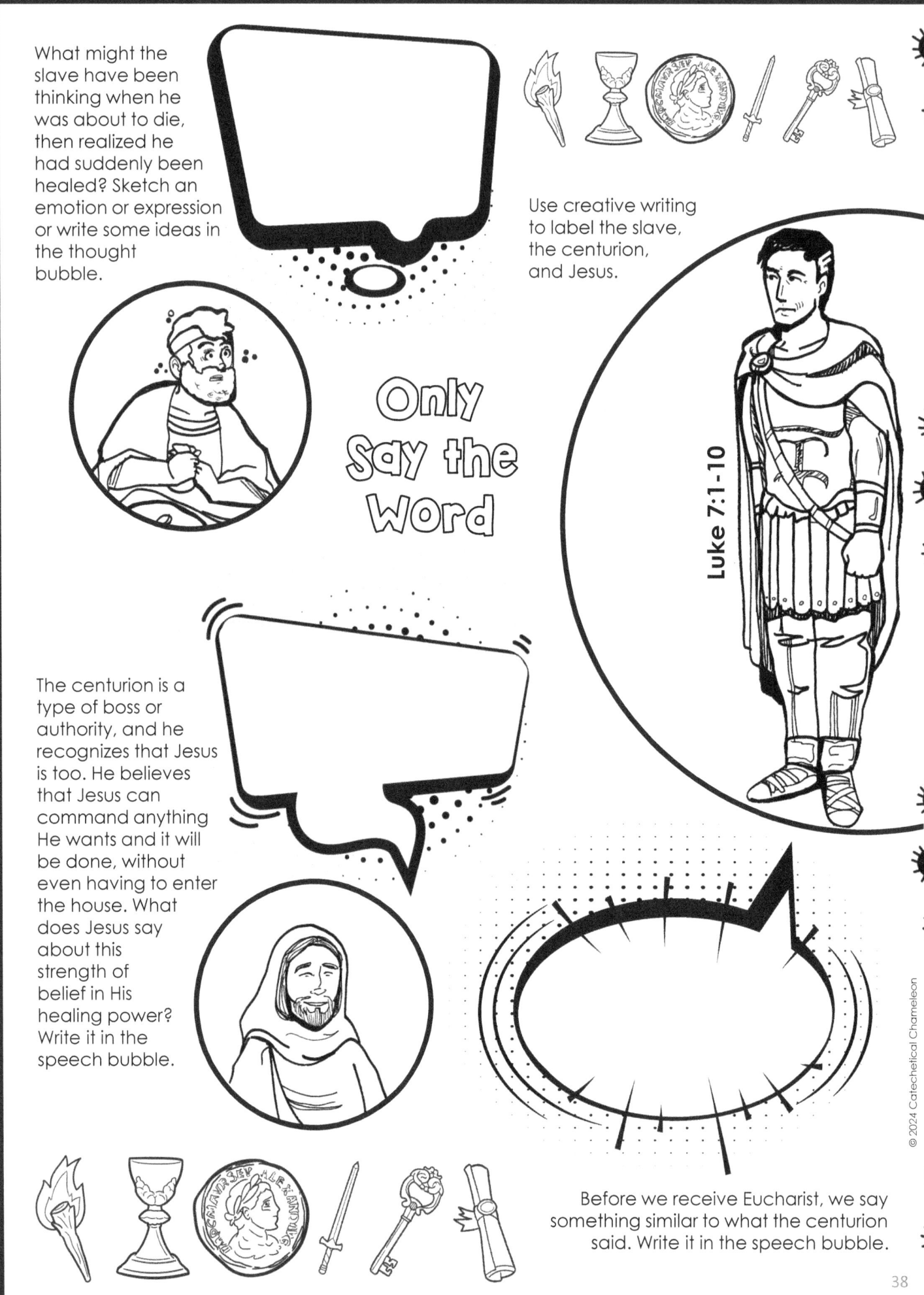

Draw the coffin in front of the weeping widow.

In this Gospel, Jesus defeats death itself (which will become a key idea later on). Design an icon or logo that represents the idea of ***conquering death***. Sketch it in the circle.

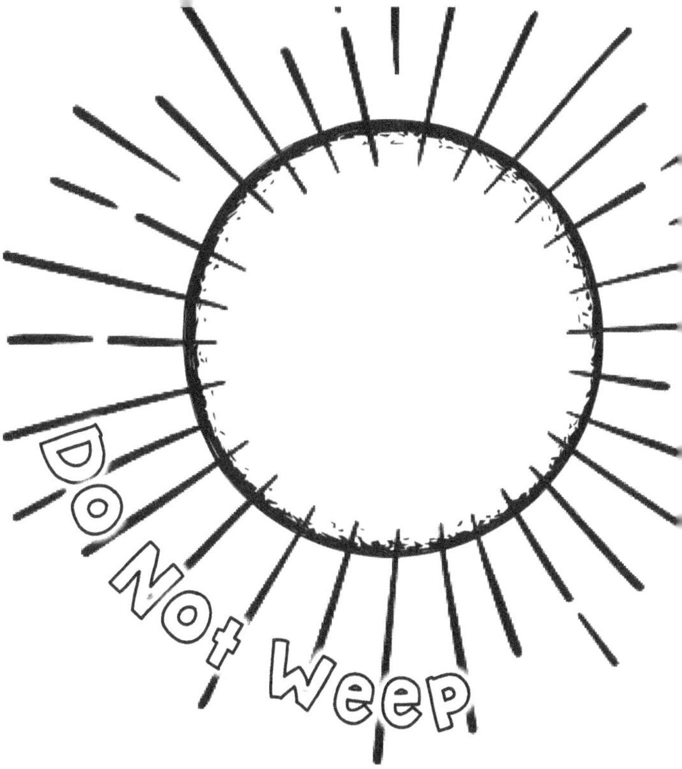
Do Not Weep

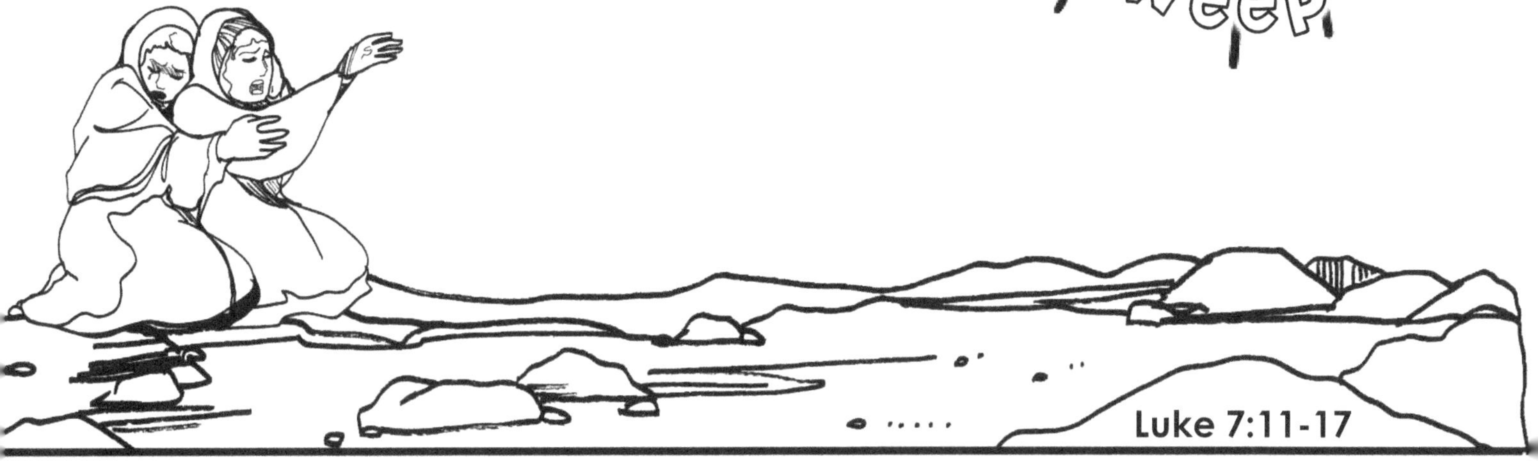
Luke 7:11-17

Use creative lettering and doodles to represent the idea of a transformation ***from death into life*** in the box below.

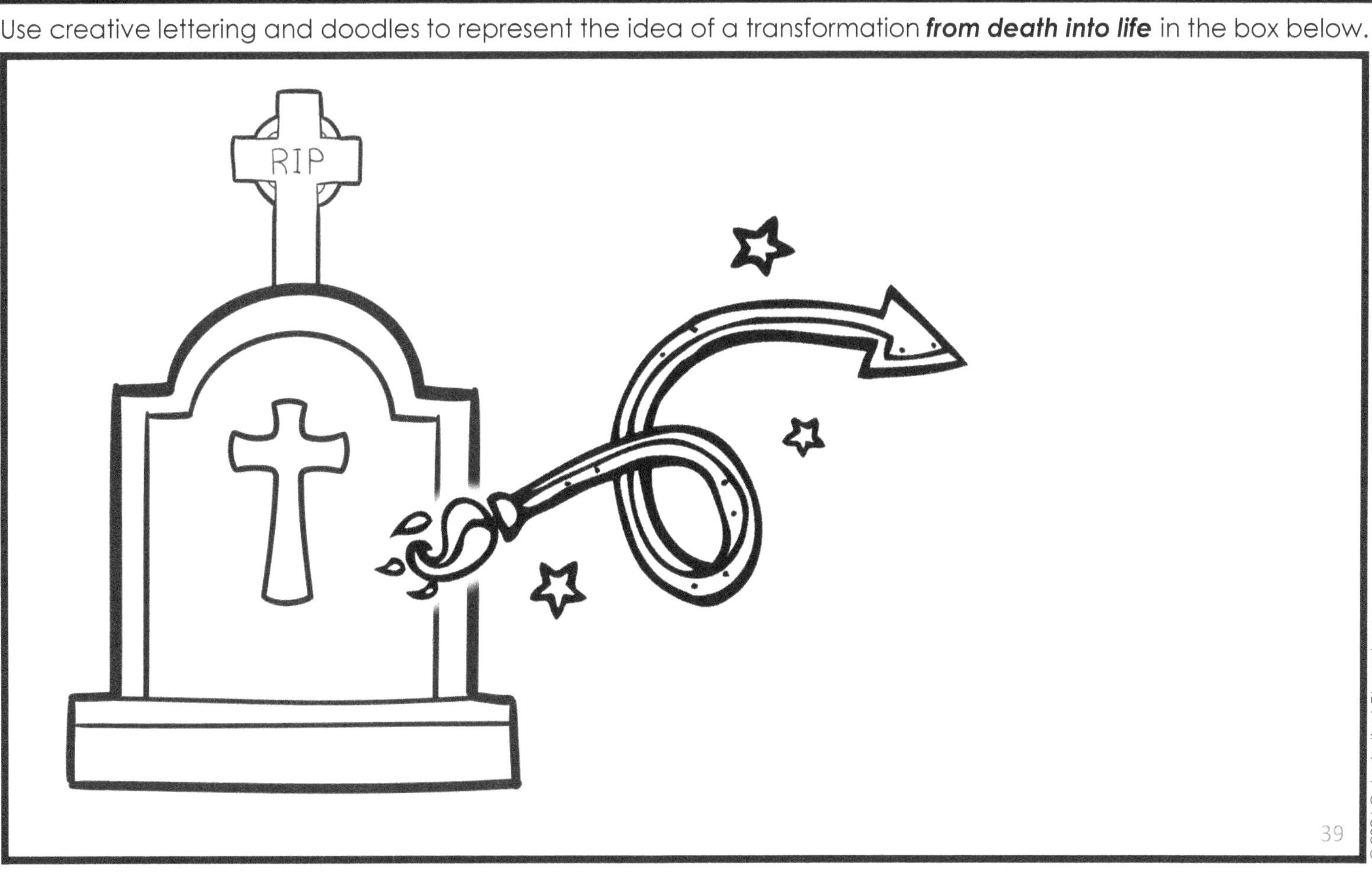
RIP

Your Sins Are Forgiven

In the boxes, use sketches and/or creative lettering to compare the Pharisee and the sinful woman. Focus on the following:

- ❑ Their status in society
- ❑ How each treats Jesus
- ❑ How Jesus treats them
- ❑ The forgiveness
- ❑ The love
- ❑ Any other key ideas that stand out to you

Luke 7:36-8:3

the Sinful Woman **VS.** *the Pharisee*

Remember the recent gospel about not being worthy? Even though we can never deserve the redemption Jesus offers us, we should accept and appreciate it. Write a short prayer reflecting on this idea below.

What could the Pharisee have done differently? What does this show us about how we should think about the forgiveness that Jesus offers to us?

© 2024 Catechetical Chameleon

Who Do You Say that I Am?

Luke 9:18-24

Look up the etymologies (origin and meaning of the words) **Christ** and **Messiah**. Show all the information that you find about the meanings of the two words below.

CHRIST

MESSIAH

 What type of savior did the Jewish people **think** they were waiting for?

 What did Jesus say about His role instead?

 What does it mean for us to **take up our cross daily**? This is the way Jesus said we must live in order to follow Him.

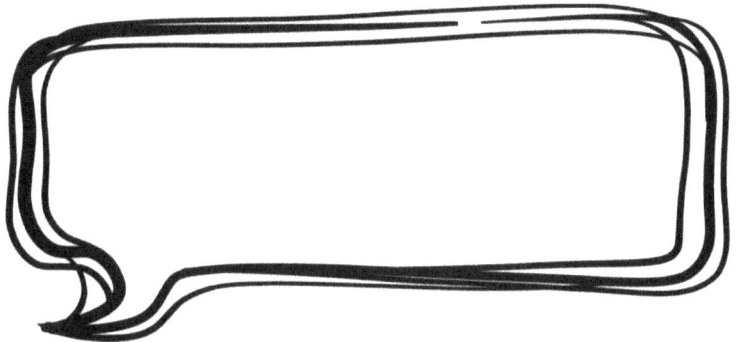

 Copy the important verse where Jesus predicts the way He will die and rise again.

Luke 9:51-62

What does the word **rebuke** mean?

Jesus rebukes the request for punishment from heaven. Why do you think He does this?

I Will Follow Wherever You Go

"Foxes have dens and birds of the sky have nests, but the Son of Man has nowhere to rest his head"

What does this mean? Sketch the nest and den, then in the third box, show what it says about Jesus's lifestyle.

Do you ever think, "Ok, Jesus, I will follow you **... but FIRST ...**" and add something in that feels more urgent? Jesus gives two more rebukes about this. Explain both examples from the Gospel. Then, quote Jesus's answers to each.

1.

2.

What do His statements mean? Use creative lettering to write up the message that we need to remember in your own words below:

Peace to this Household

Imagine you are a translator for this Gospel's message. Your job is to explain the deeper meaning to a group of people unfamiliar with this particular part of Jesus's ministry. Write the key idea below:

explain it

Then, run each of these phrases through the interpreting machine and write a translation of what they mean.

1. The kingdom of God is at hand
2. The harvest is abundant but the laborers are few
3. like lambs among wolves

interpreting machine

color it

translate it

Luke 10:1-12, 17-20

Make a slide with icons in a quick flowchart or diagram showing what Jesus was asking these pairs of people to do.

diagram it

write a short prayer about it

Martha & Mary

Inside the box below Martha, sketch some of the things she was probably focused on. In the box below Mary, sketch what she was focused on.

Which sister can you relate to more? Do you have a tendency to want to love through **serving with your hands** or to love through **socializing or listening**? Put a big checkmark in the circle under the one that feels similar to you.

Now, think of someone you know who is the opposite. Explain how they love others best, in a different way than you do.

Think of someone you know who could really use some quality time with you this week. Make a plan to spend time loving this person the way that Mary loved Christ. Write your plan here.

Luke 10:38-42

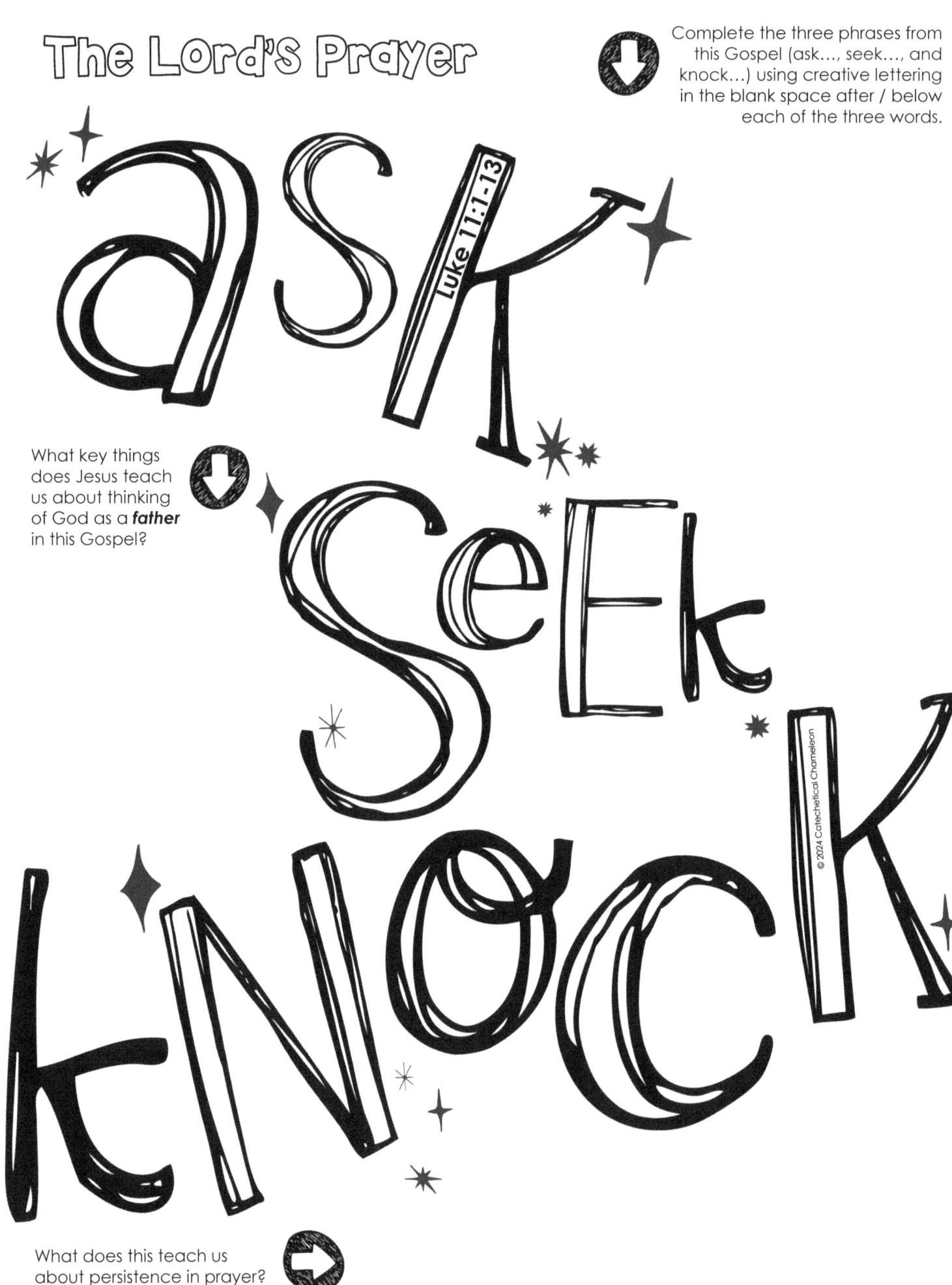

Be Prepared

What does each of these look like in someone who is **prepared** for the master, the Son of Man, to come at an hour they cannot expect? Use words or sketches to note a few bulletpoints for each. Consider not only what **is** potentially included in each category for someone prepared for Jesus, but also some ideas of what you would **not** see. Everyone's examples and ideas may be different, but use this time to reflect and consider what details should be present or not present in daily life if you are living a life prepared for Jesus. How can each of these aspects of a student's life lead Jesus to be talking about **them** when he says, "blessed is the servant…"?

- What might the **weekly schedule** of someone prepared for the Son of Man look like?
- What might the **words** of someone prepared for the Son of Man sound like?
- What might the **home or bedroom** of someone prepared for the Son of Man look like?
- What might the **social life, hobbies, parties, and activities** of someone prepared for the Son of Man look like?
- What might the **daily routine** of someone prepared for the Son of Man look like?
- What might the **internet history** of someone prepared for the Son of Man look like?

Luke 12:32-48

Add colorful flames around the image, and within them, embed some sketches and icons that show what this "fire" represents in this Gospel.

I Have Come to Set Fire

Luke 12:49-53

Inside the each half of the heart, use creative lettering to write what the two "sides" will be when a household is divided as Jesus predicts.

How can Jesus be prince of peace, but also set the earth on fire with division?

Why does Jesus's Gospel message cause division?

Give 2 examples of specific moments or situations where Jesus humbled Himself during His life on earth. Use both sketches *and* creative lettering of words / phrases to show them.

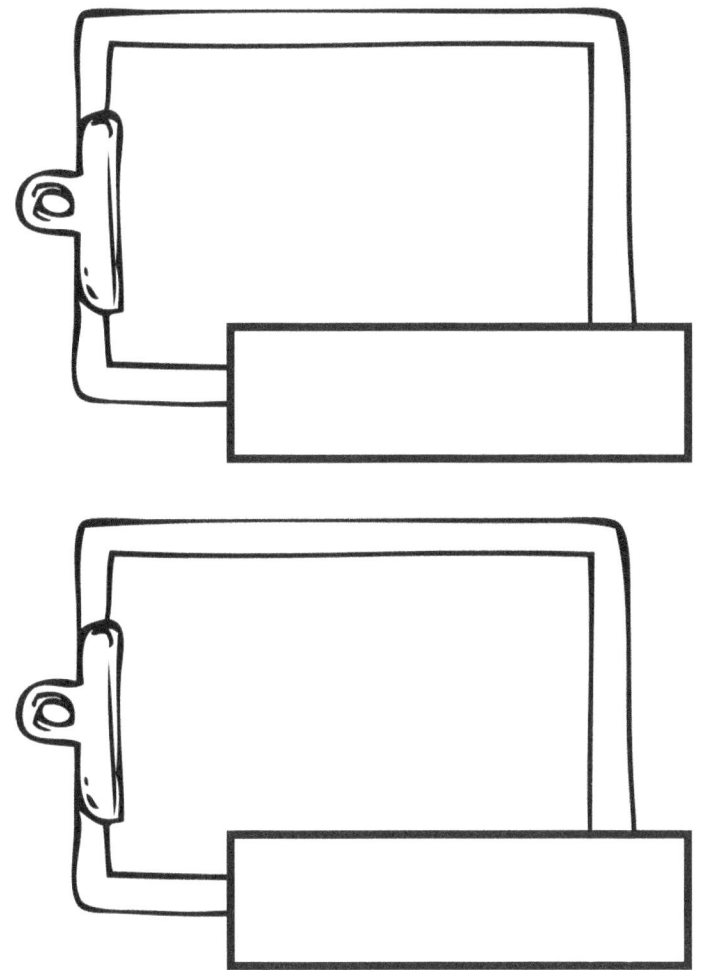

What does it look like in our daily lives to humble ourselves? Give 2 examples / situations using both drawings *and* words.

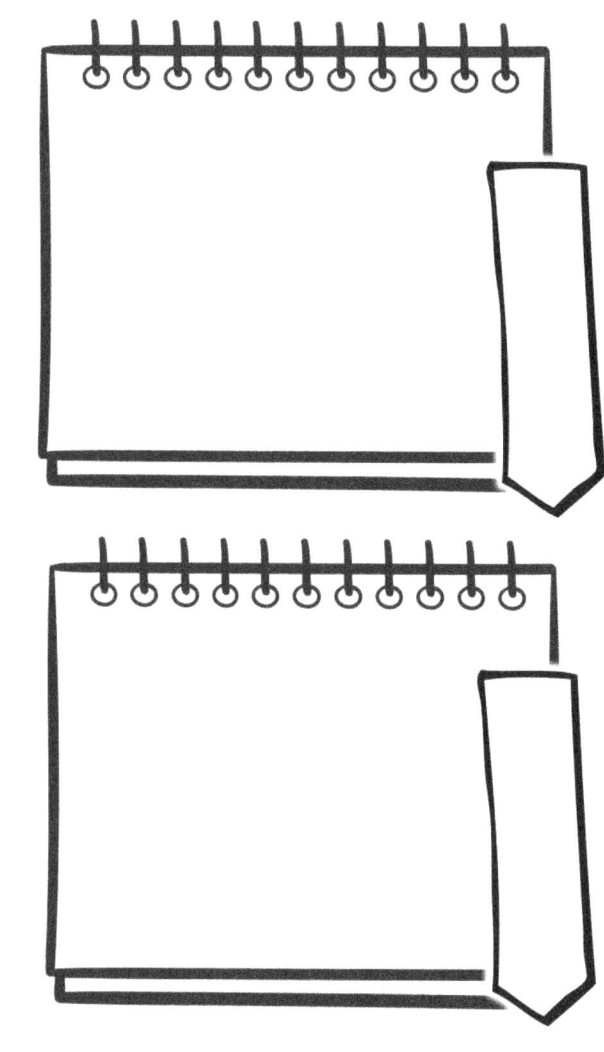

© 2024 Catechetical Chameleon

Humility & Exaltation

How does exalting yourself give you a reward *now* compared to the reward in heaven that Jesus is talking about? What is the reward?

Luke 14:1, 7-14

Parables

Luke 15:1-32

In the three circles, explain the key message behind each of the three parables.

What is a **parable**?

What do the **sinners** need to understand?

What do the **Pharisees** need to understand?

What does Jesus teach in this Gospel about things and people that are **lost**?

The Dishonest Steward

Below each of these quotes from this gospel, write a brief explanation of what it means.

Then in the TV screen, give an example of this from your own experience, the experience of someone you know, or the experience of a fictional character in a story of your imagination.

Luke 16:1-13

"The person who is trustworthy in very small matters is also trustworthy in great ones; and the person who is dishonest in very small matters is also dishonest in great ones"

"If you are not trustworthy with what belongs to another, who will give you what is yours?"

"No servant can serve two masters. He will either hate one and love the other, or be devoted to one and despise the other. You cannot serve God and mammon."

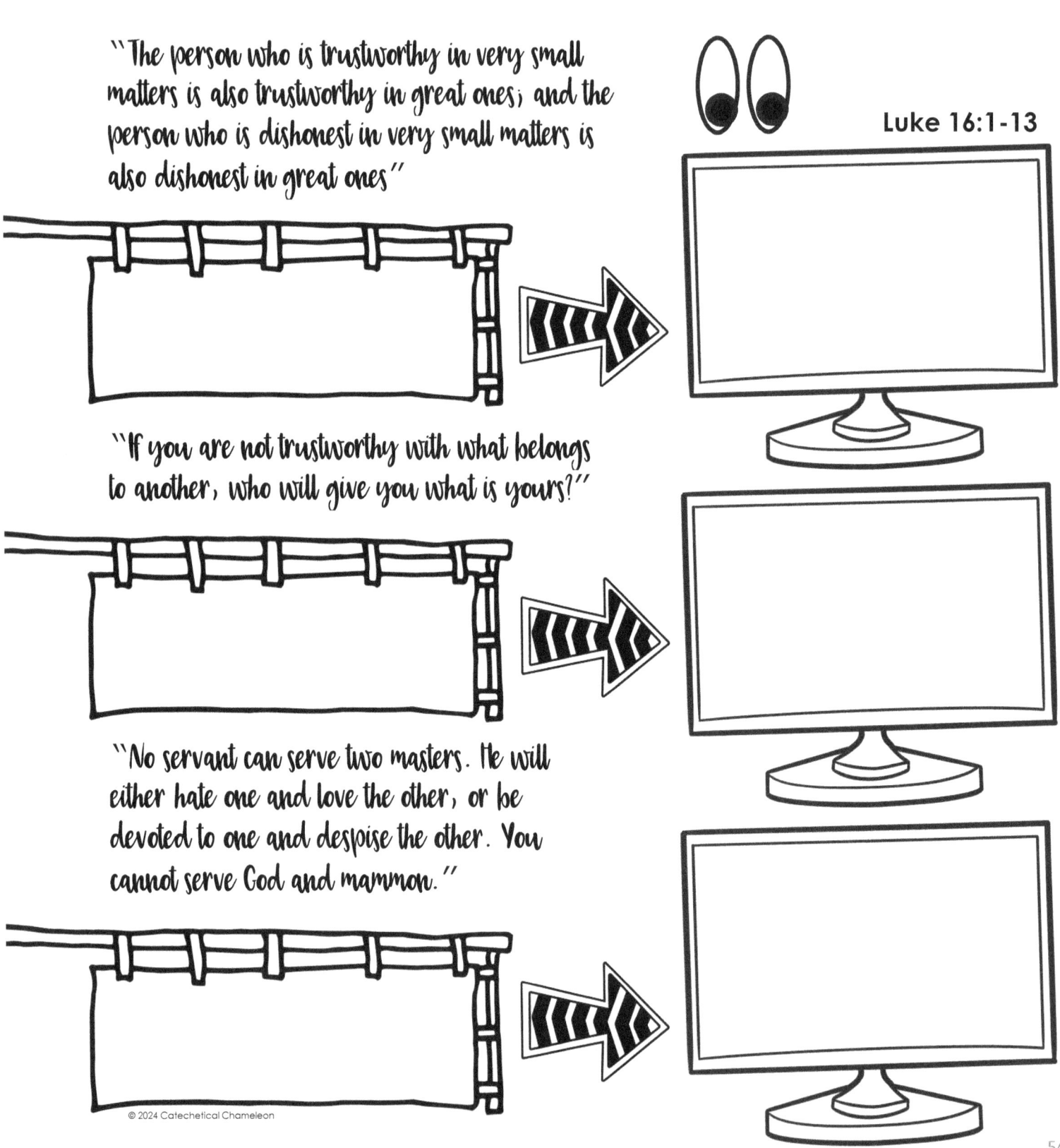

Explain Jesus's example of the *mustard seed*. What does this mean about our faith?

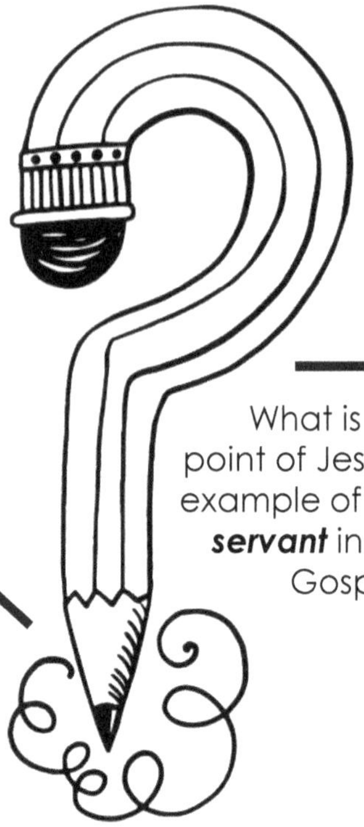

What is the point of Jesus's example of the *servant* in this Gospel?

Faith to Move Mountains

In each mountaintop, sketch or write one thing that feels like an impossible, unmovable mountain to you in this world right now.

Luke 17:5-10

Lord, increase my faith.

The Cleansing of Lepers

Luke 17:11-19

What does this gospel teach us about...

GRATITUDE

What does this gospel teach us about...

FAITH

What does this gospel teach us about...

SALVATION

© 2024 Catechetical Chameleon

Keep knocking on God's DOOR

Decorate the doors to heaven, and draw yourself, making this your own hand, knocking on it in prayer. (A stick figure is fine.) In the speech bubble, add your own prayer. Do not hesitate to *repeat* it!

Luke 18:1-8

Prayer of the Persistent Widow

Pray always without becoming WEARY

How are you doing with this challenge to **pray always** right now? Color the number of doors to match how you'd rate yourself on a scale of 1-10, then, set a goal for this week by coloring a different door further along in another color. Remember to persist daily in your prayer to reach it.

© 2024 Catechetical Chameleon

"When the Son of Man comes, will he find faith on earth?"

What do you think? Will Jesus find faith on earth when He comes again?

Pharisee vs. Tax Collector

Both people in this Gospel are imperfect sinners (as we all are), but there are some key differences. Label one circle to represent the Pharisee and one to represent the tax collector, and inside the circles, compare and contrast the two.

Luke 18:9-14

As you color, use this quote to pray for God's mercy. You can repeat it like a meditation as you add color, doodles, and embellishments.

"O God, be merciful to me, a sinner."

What are 2 things you can do to keep a *humble* attitude?

"Everyone who exalts himself will be humbled, and the one who humbles himself will be exalted."

Question About the Resurrection

Luke 20:27-38

The question in this Gospel is actually a great question, even though the Sadducees were using it here to try to disprove the existence of an eternal life beyond this earthly life. When a spouse dies and the person remarries, which spouse will they have in heaven? What surprises you most about Jesus's answer?

What are some of the main purposes of sacramental marriage?

Marriage models an example of Christ's sacrificial love for His church. Why will we not need this in heaven?

ACROSS

1. The children of God will ___.
3. Which prophet made known what would happen to the dead?
5. Who was impressed by Jesus's answer?
7. To God, all are ___.

DOWN

2. Who challenged Jesus?
3. What sacrament is not needed in the coming age?
4. What awaits God's children?
6. Like ___, they will become eternally alive.

© 2024 Catechetical Chameleon

The End of Days

How does this Gospel make you feel? Brave and ready, or worried and wanting to run or hide? Color all the icons that show how you feel inside when you read it.

Which line of this Gospel strikes you the most or triggers your imagination? Quote it here.

Luke 21:5-19

Write and say a prayer asking for Jesus to help you in times of persecution. Use the Gospel passage as a reference for the specifics that you want to ask for.

Use creative lettering and/or sketches to represent the ideas of faith vs. fear and reflect and pray as you doodle in this space about this concept.

Who instituted this feast day in the Catholic church?

hand letter it

Why was this day designated as a special day to end the liturgical year?

explain it

reflect on it

Jesus, remember me when you come into your kingdom.

Lord Jesus Christ, King of the Universe

Sketch an image of Jesus and the criminals during their last moments on earth together. (Stick figures are fine!)

Add the following details:
- ☐ The inscription above Jesus
- ☐ The soldiers and their actions
- ☐ The words of each in the speech bubbles

Luke 23:35-43

sketch it

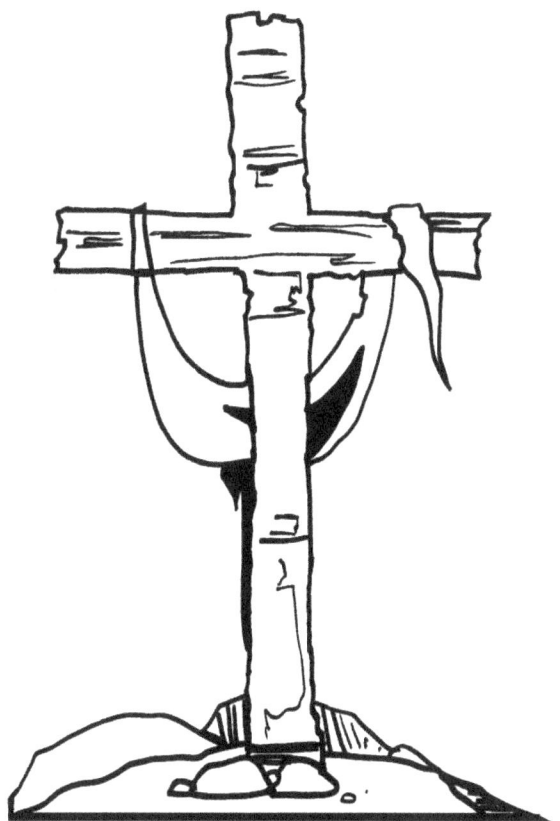

LENT

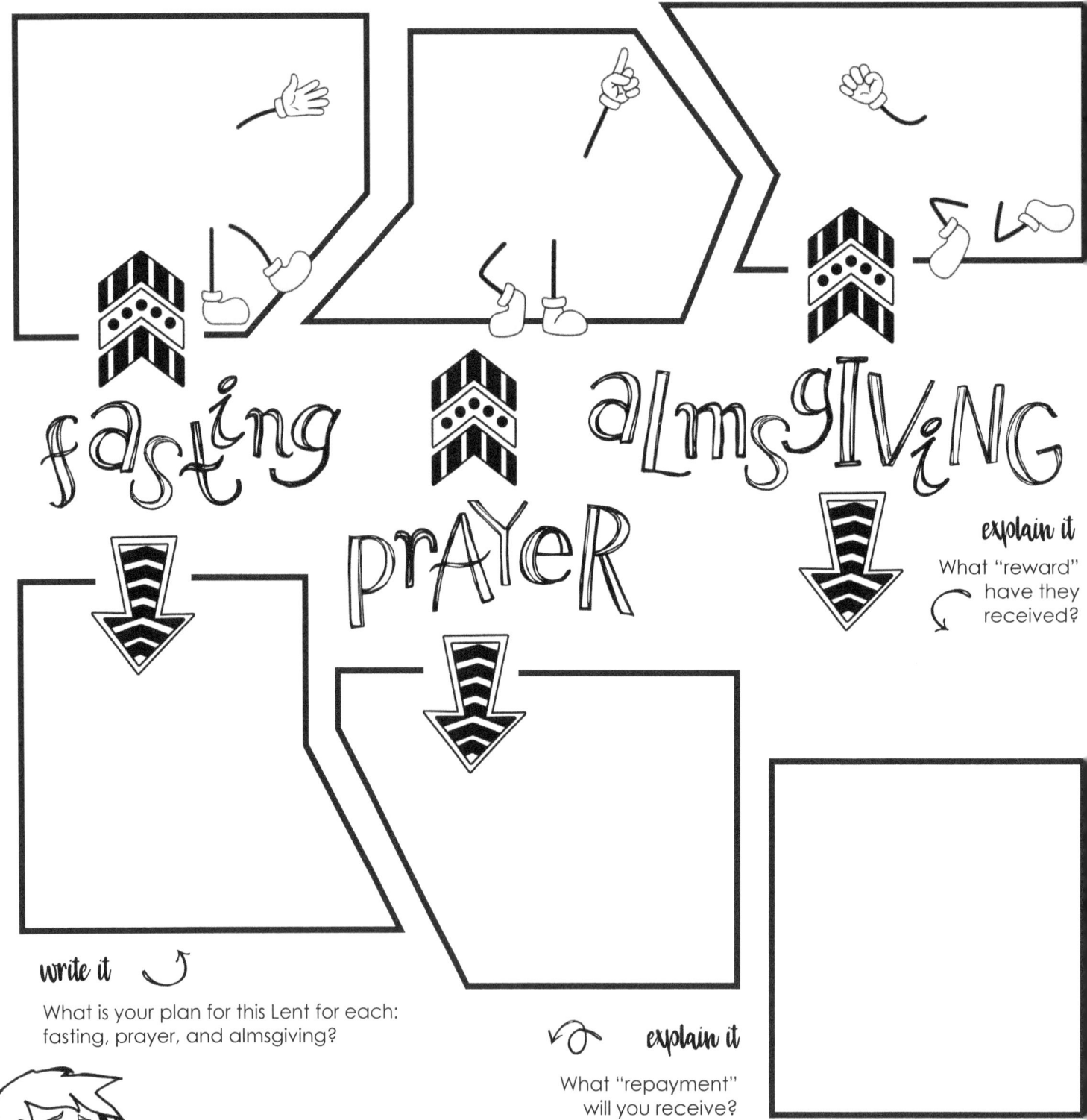

Jesus Said in Reply

At the very beginning of this Gospel, who is joining Jesus in the desert to help Him through this time of temptation? Sketch an icon or image in the circle that represents this holy companion.

Do you invite the Holy Spirit to accompany you in your own temptations? Without Him, we can get lost, but with His help we can be strong enough to resist temptation. Reflect on your most difficult temptations. In the box below, sketch a representation of one or more that you are battling lately. Then add the Holy Spirit watching over in the circle. Color while you pray about it, inviting Him to be with you to help you in those times.

Luke 4:1-13

Where else in scripture do we see the number forty? Did you know that a pregnancy is usually around 40 weeks as well? What do you think is the significance of this number? Explain.

The Transfiguration

It is revealed to just a few close friends that Jesus is surrounded with the glory of God and is claimed by God Himself as His Son.

Draw a large mountain to fill the box. Inside it, use creative lettering to write the significance of the mountain. (If you are not sure, think back to other important moments in the Bible that happen on a mountaintop.)

On top of the mountain, add Jesus, surrounded in imagery that represents the glory of God.

In the space below, write a short prayer about God's glory and His plans for Jesus's "exodus that he was going to accomplish in Jerusalem."

Luke 9:28-36

© 2024 Catechetical Chameleon

The tragedies that Jesus references at the beginning of this gospel remind the people that time can be limited. Any suffering or death of a person does not signify their own sin. He clarifies that while still using these examples as a reminder that we must repent from our sins. Without repentence, He says, we shall perish as they did.

Repentance and Bearing Fruit

Luke 13:1-9

Imagine you are the fig tree, with only **one more chance** to bear fruit.

What does it mean to "bear fruit" symbolically? Explain here. Then inside the fruits, show what that might look like in the life of someone who is repentant and is following Jesus. Use either creative lettering or sketches to give your specific examples in each fruit.

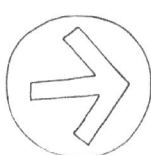

What can you nourish your roots with to grow closer to God and bear that symbolic fruit? Explain here, and then add sketches or hand lettering in the soil around the roots to show some examples.

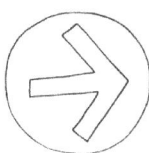

write it

Which character can you understand or relate to most? Explain why.

The Prodigal Son

Luke 15:1-3, 11-32

© 2024 Catechetical Chameleon

Which of these happens in this gospel? Color yes or no to identify which events are included.

- The father gives the younger son his inheritance.
- The younger son manages the money well.
- The son eats the swine while working on the farm.
- The son realizes he has sinned against his father and God.
- The father punishes his son upon his return.
- The older son reacted the same way the father did.

color yes/no

explain it

What does this story represent? What does it teach us about God?

sketch it

Draw an icon that blends the concept of **repentance** with the idea of **forgiveness**. Design it like a logo that blends these two things together into one graphic and sketch it here.

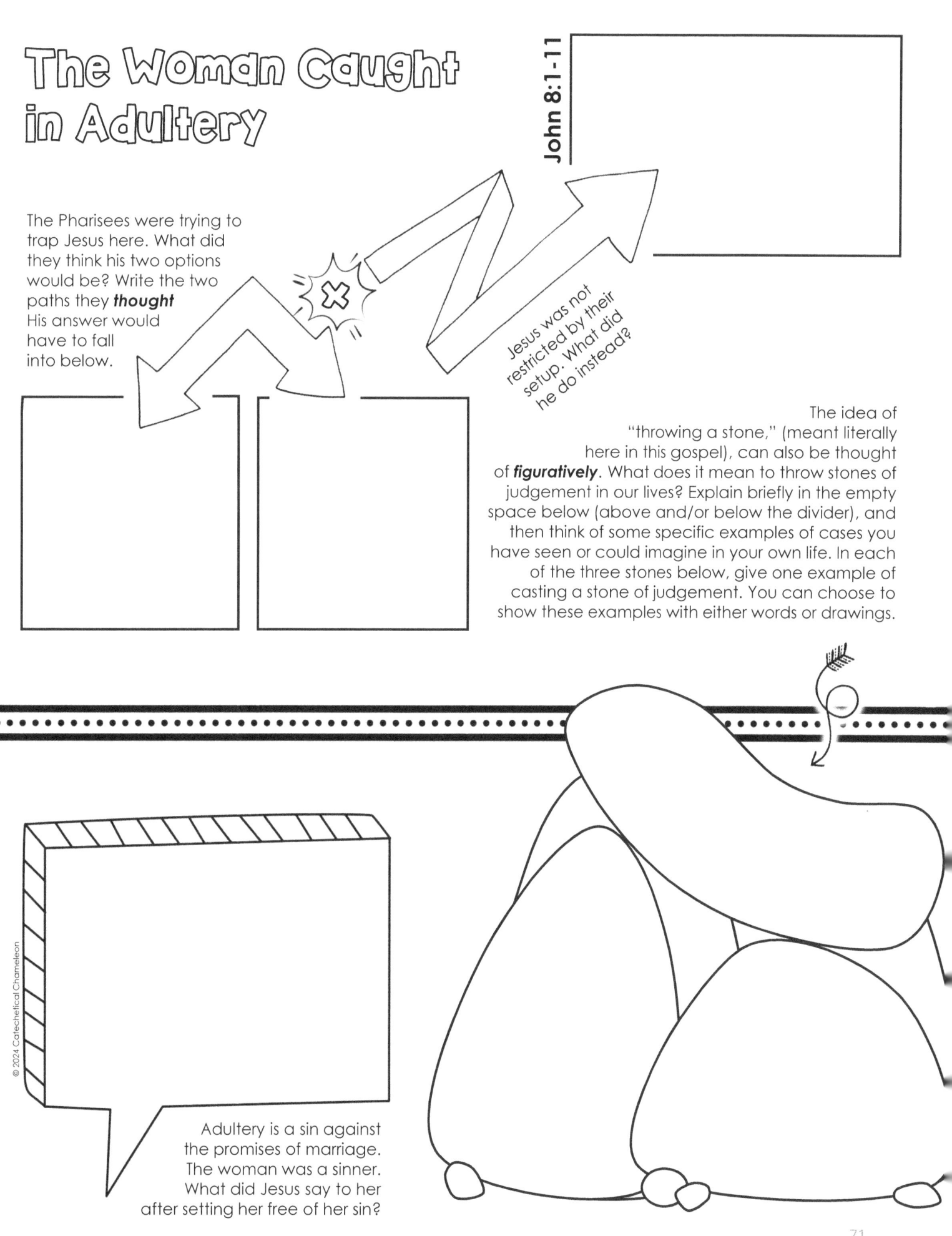

The Passion of the Lord

draw it

Draw a gift box or gift bag around the Eucharist and decorate it while you pray a prayer of thanks to Jesus for the gift of His most precious body and blood.

explain it:

What does Passover remember as a Jewish celebration?

What is the significance of the Passover Lamb in relation to Jesus's sacrifice?

SPOILER ALERTS

Luke 22:14-23:56

Sketch it

Use sketches or words with creative lettering to show what Jesus is revealing about the future with each of these statements:

1. "I have eagerly desired to eat this Passover with you before I suffer."

2. "From this time on I shall not drink of the fruit of the vine until the kingdom of God comes."

3. "This is my body, which will be given for you."

4. "The hand of the one who is to betray me is with me on the table."

5. "I tell you, Peter, before the cock crows this day, you will deny three times that you know me."

SNEAK PEEKS

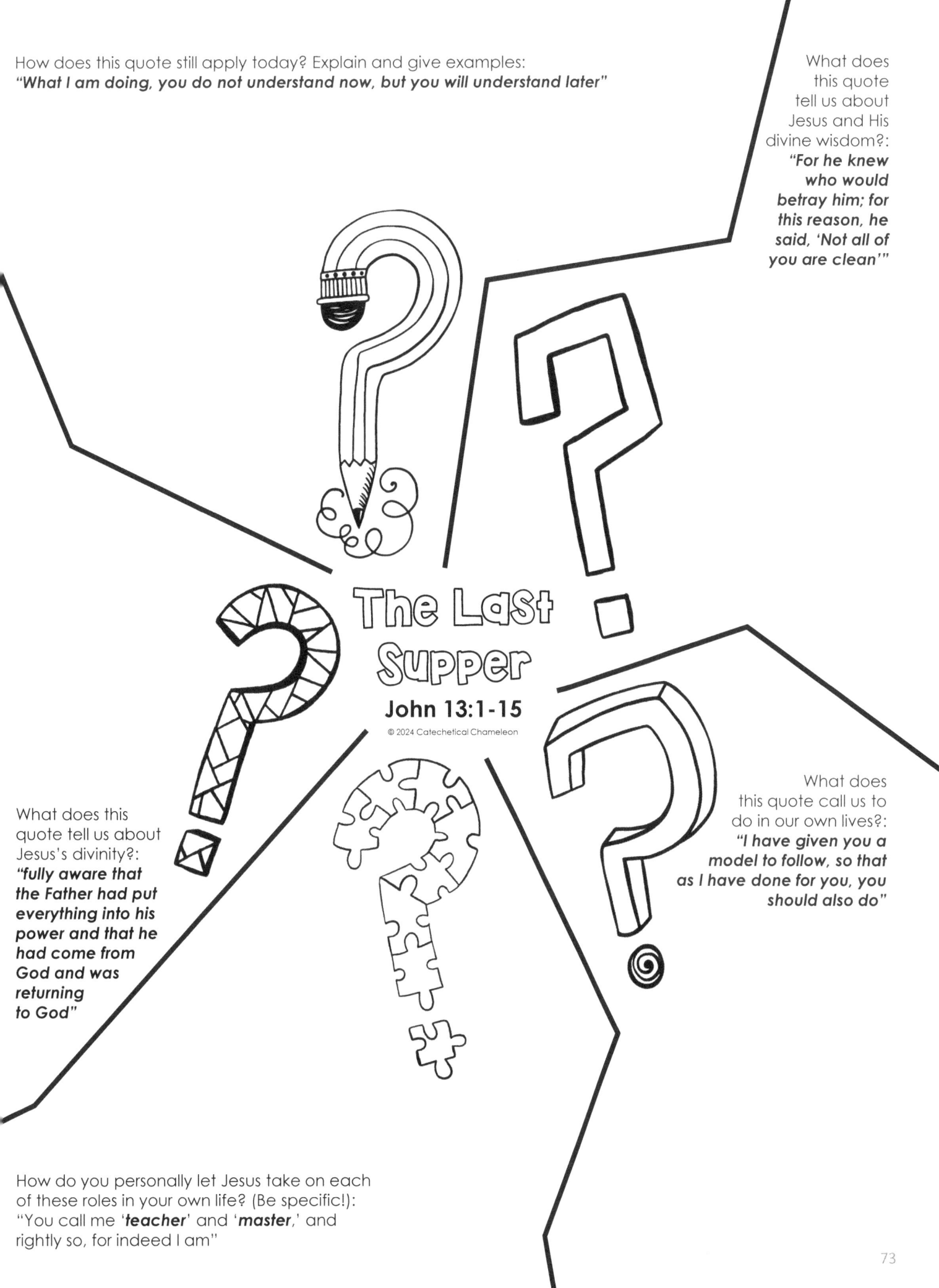

How does this quote still apply today? Explain and give examples:
"What I am doing, you do not understand now, but you will understand later"

What does this quote tell us about Jesus and His divine wisdom?:
"For he knew who would betray him; for this reason, he said, 'Not all of you are clean'"

What does this quote tell us about Jesus's divinity?:
"fully aware that the Father had put everything into his power and that he had come from God and was returning to God"

What does this quote call us to do in our own lives?:
"I have given you a model to follow, so that as I have done for you, you should also do"

How do you personally let Jesus take on each of these roles in your own life? (Be specific!):
*"You call me '**teacher**' and '**master**,' and rightly so, for indeed I am"*

The Last Supper
John 13:1-15
© 2024 Catechetical Chameleon

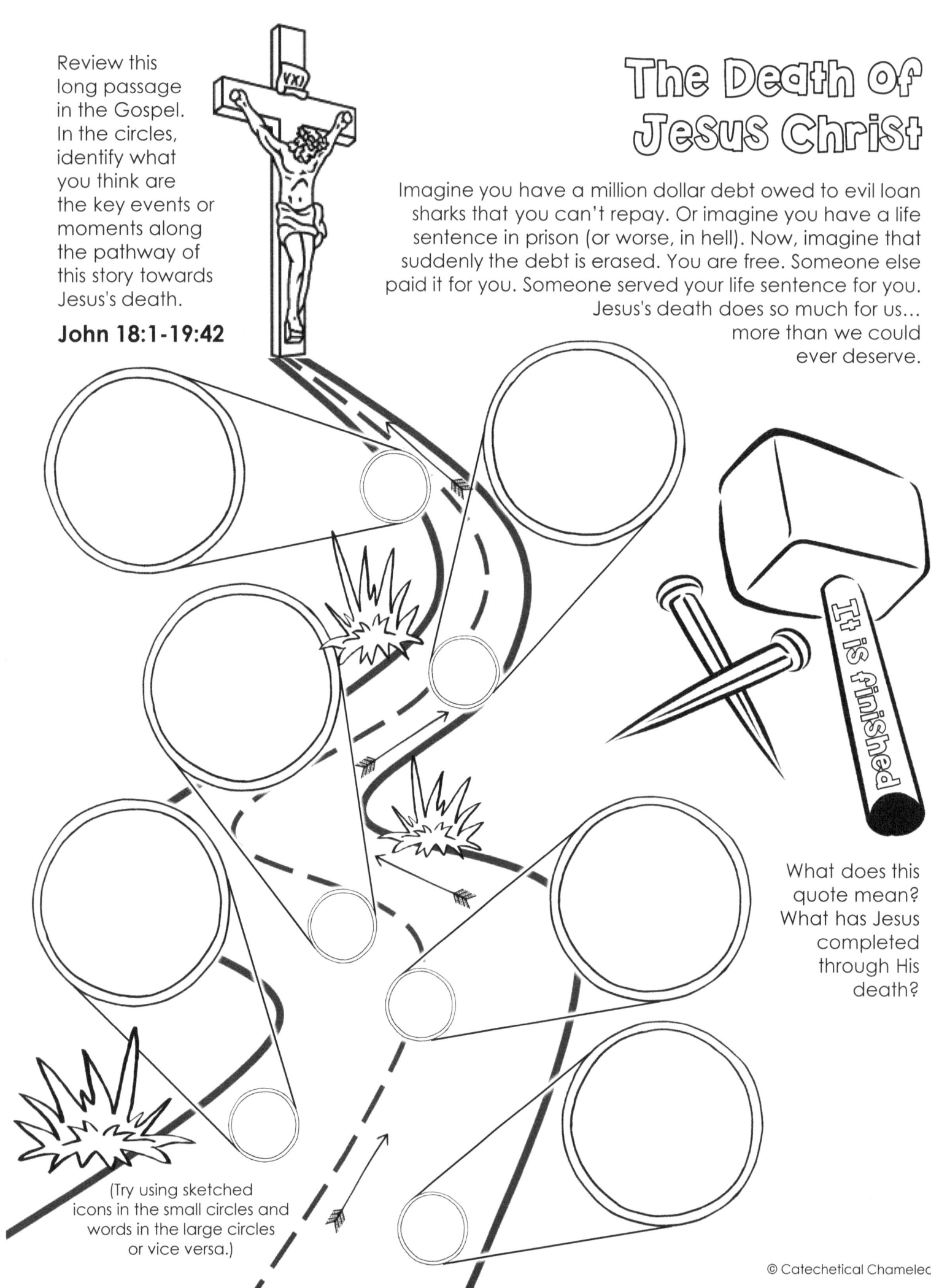

John 20:19-31

The presence of Jesus brings us many gifts. Starting with "peace," use creative lettering to list a few more nouns that God offers us through Jesus.

Peace

Peace Be With You

from *fear* into FAITH

"Have you come to believe because you have seen me? Blessed are those who have not seen and have believed."

| What makes you feel afraid? | God frequently says to "**NOT** be afraid." What are some strategies that we can use in moments of fear to shift from the mindset of fear into the mindset of faith? | Write a short prayer that Jesus will help you believe in Him without seeing in the same way the apostles did. |

© 2024 Catechetical Chameleon

John 21:1-19

What is Jesus calling **Peter** to do when he says "follow me."?

Doodle in a colorful way inside the arrow while reflecting on this Gospel and praying about following Jesus.

What is Jesus calling **you** to do when he says "follow me."?

How does Jesus show **the disciples** that they can have faith in Him and trust that they will be ok even when following Him might seem scary?

How does Jesus show **you** that you can have faith in Him and trust that **you** will be ok even when following Him might seem scary?

How do you choose people (other than Jesus) to "follow"? If you were to follow someone online or in your life, what would you be looking for to help you make the decision to follow? Sketch an image of someone who would be worthy of following. Explain why.

Follow Me

follow me

© 2024 Catechetical Chameleon

Have you ever noticed that parents are happy when their children get along well, and they get upset when the siblings fight? How does this truth help us understand this new commandment from Jesus? How does loving **one another** show **God** glory and fulfill God's will?

Love One Another

Fill it in with creative lettering:

This is how all will know that you are my

_____

if you have love for one another.

```
P Y T L I S E U L N O C H C E
B G C O A M E R D F E A M W H
J O T N E M D N A M M O C U O
E E D G R E I S N B M P L O T
S C U E D T H J E L I J S G N
U L M R D I S C I P L E S S B
S B O A S E L O H T A S O D Q
V M N V A N I M Z K W I T N E
R J D L E R I F E C A Y D O A
L N A K I T C H I L D R E N L
C O M M Y V O L C R E L J I G
F S R A S D Y T D A O M A M X
O C E I A O K H J S E L C K R
Q T D L F G E N A M M O G T I
R R A V O M C L A R E S S A D
```

Find ten words (with 3 or more letters) from this Gospel passage hidden in the grid above.

 Research St. Thomas Aquinas's definition of **love** and write it here.

80

Peace Be With You

John 20:19-23

The disciples receive the peace of the Holy Spirit (and so do we) to go from **fear** to **bold bravery**, and from **wimps** to **warriors** who will go spread the Gospel.

When we allow the grace of the Holy Spirit into our lives, the twelve fruits of the Spirit become visible in us. Look up the meaning of each of the twelve fruits of the Holy Spirit so that you can label them in the vertical banners on the squares to the right and sketch an icon that represents each one in the square. →

gifts of the Holy Spirit

fruits of the Holy Spirit

The Holy Spirit showers us with good gifts. Look up the meaning of each of the seven gifts of the Holy Spirit so that you can label them in the rims of the coins and sketch an icon that represents each one on the coin faces. ←

HOLY DAYS

Immaculate Conception

The Feast of the Immaculate Conception is about how **one** of these two was conceived. Color only that one.

color it

Define "immaculate." *define it*

Sketch it
Design a logo / icon above that combines two images to represent the special blend of ***perfection*** and ***motherhood*** that made Mary so special.

Luke 1:26-38

© 2024 Catechetical Chameleon

86

BONUS PAGES

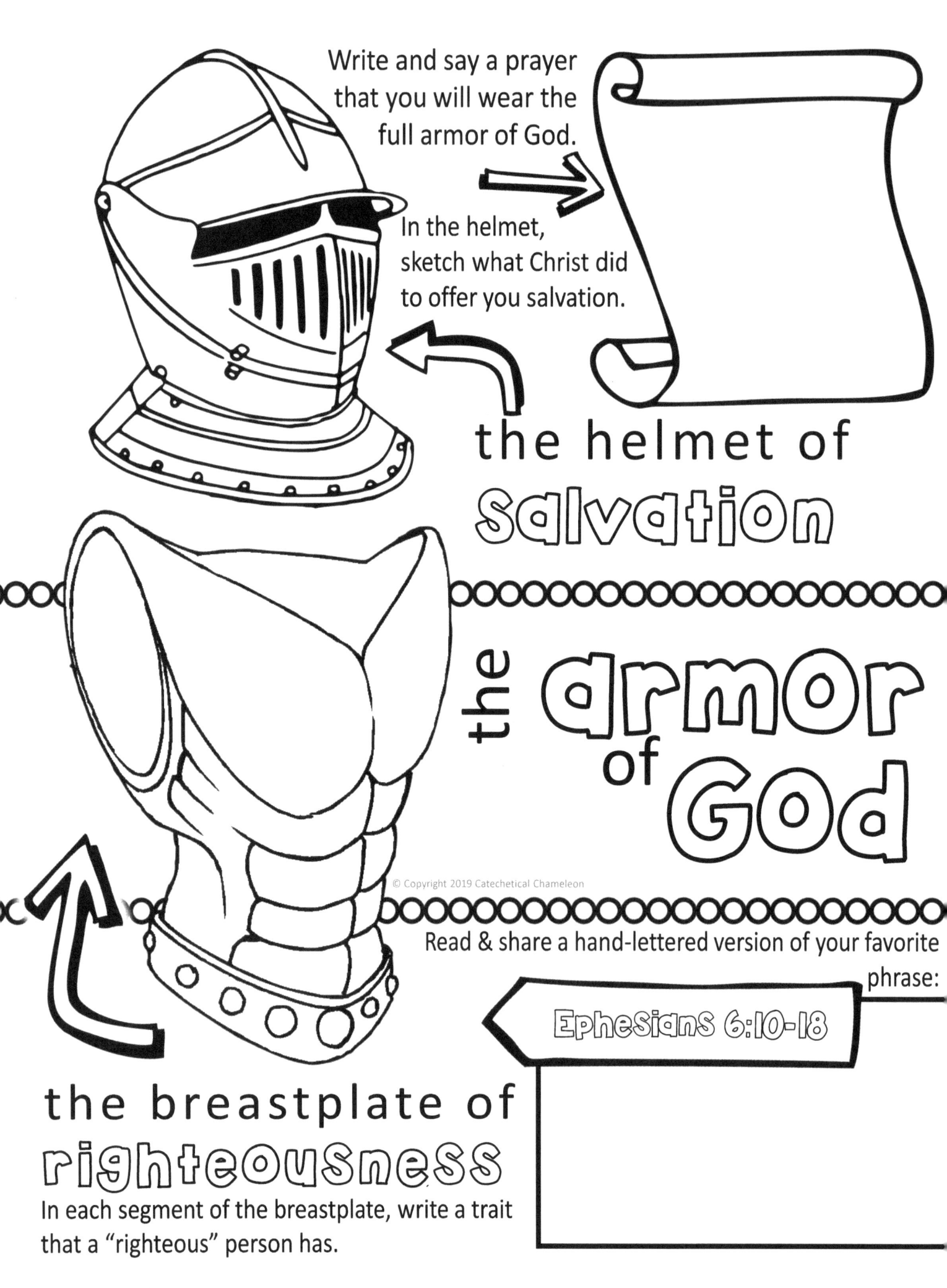

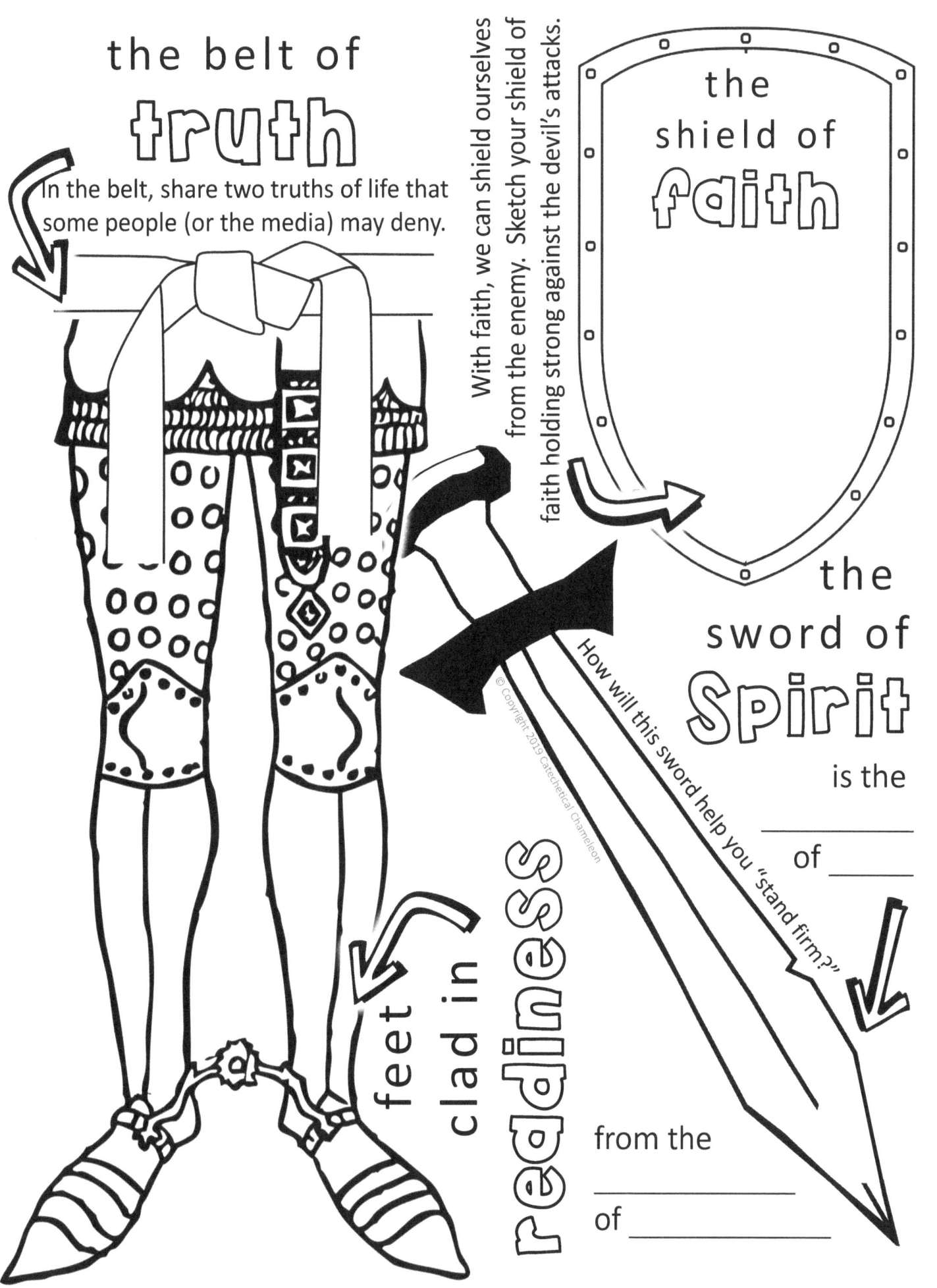

- ☐ Color the words around the perimeter of the calendar using the color listed.
- ☐ Fill in the blanks to show what each color represents.
- ☐ Write the season of the church year inside each sector.
- ☐ Show the seasons of the regular calendar year outside of the circle.

Name:

The Liturgical Calendar

SUNDAY GOSPELS
CYCLE YEAR "C"

doodle
notebook
teacher guide

INTRO TO THE GOSPELS

Teacher Notes: Gospel Doodle Reflections Cycle Year "C"

INTRO

The Gospels

Background information: The word "Gospel" is from the Greek for "good tidings" or "good news." The Gospels tell the story of Jesus's life, ministry, and death. These historical documents offer 4 different perspectives of the events. They were written by men named Matthew, Mark, Luke, and John.

Timeline: Jesus was born between 6 BC and 4 BC, and began His ministry and teaching when He was around 30 years old. His death was between 30 and 36 AD. Almost 40 years after that (probably sometime around approximately 70AD), Mark wrote his account of Jesus's life. Matthew's account was written sometime between 75 and 90 AD. Luke wrote his between 80 and 95, AD, and John wrote his after 95 AD.

Help students reflect: Why is it important that we have 4 different accounts of the same historical events? What is the point of reading the Gospel? Why do we still study these texts thousands of years later?

The 4 Evangelists

Background information: The 4 different Gospel writers each wrote for a slightly different audience, and had a different perspective. We honor these men as saints.

Summary: Matthew was Jewish (like Jesus) but was greatly disliked by the Jewish people because he worked as a tax collector for the Roman government. Jesus passed by his tax collection booth and called him to "follow" Him, and Matthew did! He is often represented with an image / icon of an angel. Matthew's audience was primarily those who were already Jewish.

Mark met Jesus when he was a young boy. He writes a fast-paced, exciting account of the events that occurred. It's a short Gospel compared to the others. His symbol is a lion. He spoke to the Romans, with emphasis on action and power.

Luke's gospel is long and detailed. It focuses more than the others on Mary and the Nativity and also on Jesus healing people. Luke is represented by an ox. His audience included the Greeks, who focused on culture, beauty, and truth.

John was a young apostle, and his Gospel is more poetic. It is written more in a mystical, heavenly way, and is sometimes more symbolic. His symbol is an eagle because his Gospel is less "grounded" and soars above the earthly things. John's Gospel was written for *everyone*!

Teacher Notes: Gospel Doodle Reflections Cycle Year "C"

Scripture Citations

Background information: The Bible is a collection of many books. The Old Testament includes stories from before Jesus was born. The New Testament includes accounts of Jesus's life and beyond.

Citing Scripture: To find a passage to read, you first find the book within the Bible (in the example shown, we would find the Gospel of Luke). Then, within that book, you can reference the chapter and verses to read the correct section. The book and chapter number come before the colon, and the number of the line to start reading comes right after the colon. If there's more than one verse to read, the ending verse will be listed too. Occasionally, a passage crosses into another chapter. You may have a citation that lists one chapter and verse, then continues through another chapter and verse. Just remember that the colon placement is always (chapter): (verse(s)).

Help students reflect: What special prayer is being introduced in the beginning of Chapter 11 of Luke's Gospel? Isn't it so incredible that this prayer that we still use today comes straight from Jesus's own teaching?
In John's Gospel, Chapters 18 and 19 are the account of how Jesus died. We would probably be most likely to hear this part during Holy Week.
Take a few moments on your own to flip through the Bible. Can you find a passage somewhere in the Bible that feels relevant to you today? How would you cite the line(s) if you wanted to remember where to find them to read again, or if you wanted to share them with a friend?

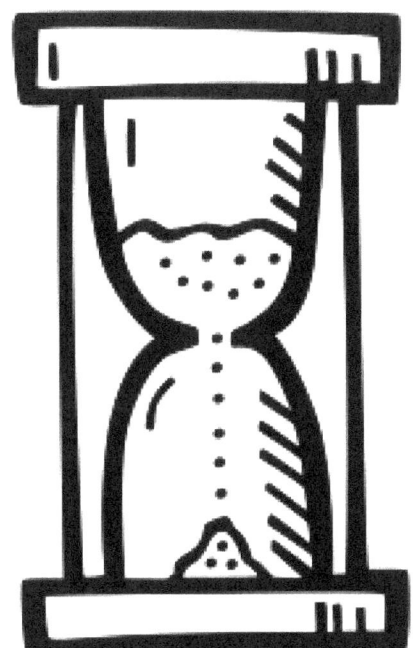

ADVENT

Teacher Notes: Gospel Doodle Reflections **Cycle Year "C"**

The Coming of the Son of Man

ADVENT

1st Sunday of Advent
Luke 21:25-28, 34-36

Background information:
- The powers of the heavens were thought to be cosmic armies of angels in ancient times.[1]
- The appearance of Jesus was foretold by the prophet Daniel and described in detail in the Book of Revelation.

Summary: Jesus tells us that He is going to come again in glory. He tells us directly that it is not going to be a pretty sight. The whole world will be confused, and people will die just from the fear. But Jesus says we should not be afraid of His coming. Instead, by avoiding sinfulness in our day-to-day life we can make ourselves ready. Jesus tells us to stand tall and accept the salvation that He offers us.

Help students reflect: How does this passage make you feel? Does it make sense for Jesus to come again in judgement? Is that too severe? Or does it make sense for God to value good character? Why is this time during Advent, preparing for Christmas, a good time to be reminded that Jesus will come again? What are we really preparing for when we prepare for Christmas? Other than the examples given in this passage, what are some ways we can prepare for the coming of Jesus?

Make Straight His Paths

2nd Sunday of Advent
Luke 3:1-6

Background information:
- Luke describes the Roman system of governance in which the Jewish priesthood was underneath the Tetrarchs (kind of like mayors), who were underneath the governors, who were underneath Caesar, the emperor. This was the system of Roman occupation of Jerusalem, an occupation the Jews did not appreciate.
- John the Baptist is supposed to remind us of the behavior of the Old Testament prophets.
- Around the time of Jesus, Jews generally did not think that their Messiah would save the Gentiles (non-Jews). Here, Luke quotes from Isaiah suggesting that the salvation of the Messiah will be for everyone (all flesh shall see...).

Summary: After establishing the historical context, Luke tells us that John the Baptist travels the whole Jordan region preaching the preparation of the Messiah: baptism, repentance, and forgiveness of sins. John the Baptist suggests that the salvation of Jesus is for everyone.

Help students reflect: Why do you think historical dates were so important to Luke? John the Baptist was a radical. Do you know any other examples of people who have given their lives so radically to God? How does our baptism (of repentance for the forgiveness of sins) prepare us to receive Jesus into our lives? How does Jesus help everyone: Christian or not?

Teacher Notes: Gospel Doodle Reflections　　　　　　　　　　　　　　　**Cycle Year "C"**

Filled with Expectation

ADVENT

3rd Sunday of Advent
Luke 3:10-18

Background information:
- Tax collectors often demanded more of the Jews than what was prescribed under Roman law. To make matters worse, in Jerusalem the tax collectors working for Rome were often Jews themselves (like Matthew).
- Roman soldiers were essentially allowed to conscribe Jews for help at will.
- "Spirit and fire" are supposed to call to mind their refining quality as well as Baptism and Confirmation and the moral conversion necessary for these sacraments.[2]

Summary: Luke tells us about John the Baptist's preaching to show us the sense of expectation that Israel had for the Messiah. Many thought that John the Baptist might be the Messiah. He made it clear that the Messiah was coming to bring God's saving presence to them. He also talked about the judgement that the Messiah would bring and the need for moral conversion.

Help students reflect: Where do we need to expect a Messiah? What needs to be "saved" in the world today? John the Baptist tells people to change their behavior and be good to others. How does changing our behavior help to prepare us for the salvation we seek? What kinds of things do we do that we need to change before Jesus arrives this Christmas?

The Visitation of Mary

4th Sunday of Advent
Luke 1:39-45

Background information:
- This scene occurs immediately after the Angel Gabriel invites Mary to be the mother of the Messiah. The Annunciation occurs after Gabriel prophecies the birth of John the Baptist to Zechariah, who doubts and consequently has his speech taken away.
- Elizabeth is married to Zechariah who had his voice taken away, but will get it back when John the Baptist is born.
- Mary and Elizabeth are cousins.

Summary: Mary makes a long journey to visit her cousin Elizabeth and celebrate their pregnancies. When she finally reaches Elizabeth, Elizabeth gives great praise to Mary's faith and the way that Mary has been honored by God for believing in His promises.

Help students reflect: This is a great scene in the Bible on the theme of friendship. What sometimes holds us back from celebrating with our friends? How can we be more like Mary and Elizabeth and put our friendships first in life? Elizabeth points out the greatness of Mary's faith. How can we trust in God more this week before Christmas? What are some faith-building exercises? Can you identify the areas of your life that are challenging your faith in God's promises? How can you work on faith in those areas?

Filled with Expectation

Luke 3:10-18

Compare the two. What is the cleansing power of water vs. the purifying property of fire? What does water represent? What does fire represent? Explain (both literally and spiritually) to tell what this means in this Gospel.

baptism with water

Water cleans. It can wash away dirt and refresh something. Our Baptisms wash away the stain of original sin and give us a refreshed new life in Christ.

One mightier than I is coming!

baptism with fire

Fire can purify, like with metals. You can melt and mold with fire. We are Purified by the Holy Spirit and we want to be molded to conform to god's will.

To separate good produce from waste, a farmer would sort the good from the bad with a winnowing fan. It was a tool that was a cross between a fork and a shovel. By using it to toss the wheat into the air, the farmer could separate the wheat from the chaff. The kernels of wheat (good) would fall to the ground to gather. The lighter chaff (bad/waste) would be blown by the wind and then collected and burned up. Reflect on the meaning of this Gospel, and find the deeper meaning of what John says the Messiah will do. Then write and say a prayer asking God's help based on your realizations.

Find the meaning:

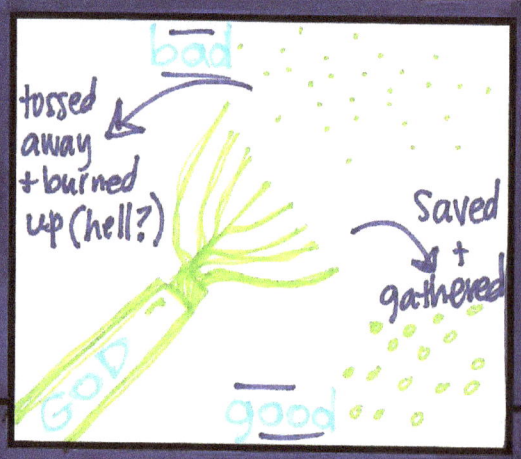

- bad — tossed away + burned up (hell?)
- GOD
- good
- Saved + gathered

Write a prayer:

Lord,
Help me to hear your word and live in a way so that I become like the wheat and not the chaff. Let me be worthy of being gathered into your kingdom + not be tossed and burned. Amen.

© 2024 Catechetical Chameleon

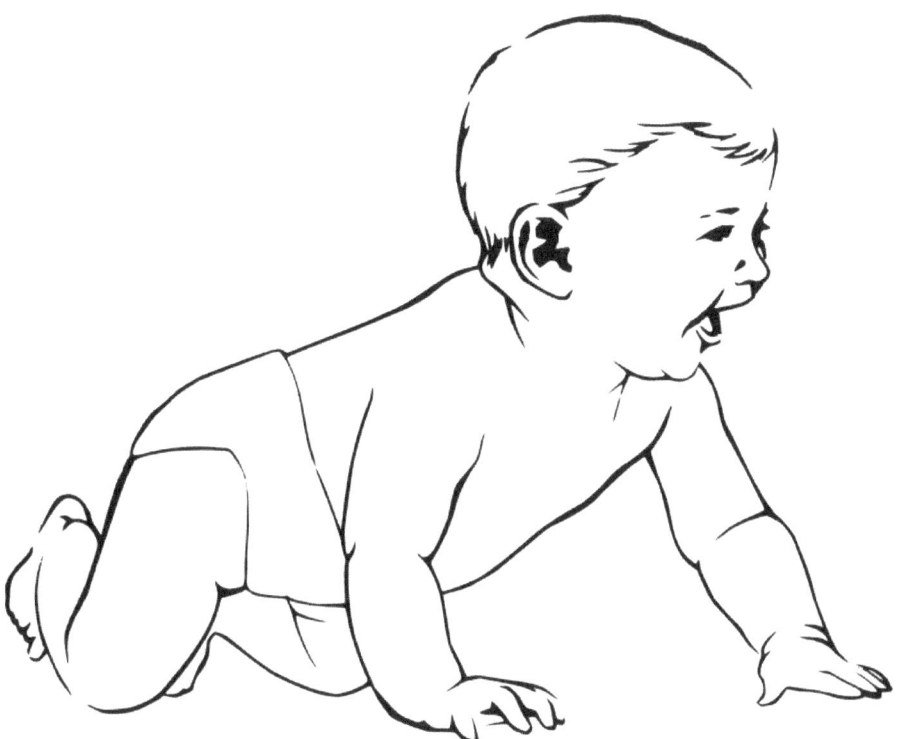

CHRISTMAS

Teacher Notes: Gospel Doodle Reflections Cycle Year "C"

The Birth of Jesus

Christmas Vigil
Matthew 1:1-25

Background information:
- Jesus's genealogy ties him to the expectation of the Messiah (David) and to the promise of blessing on every nation (Abraham). It is also unusual for its time because it includes women.
- Many of the people in Jesus's family tree sinned famously.
- Betrothal meant the commitment of marriage without living together for several months before normal married life began; it is like engagement, but more committed.
- Jewish law called for adulterers to be stoned. Joseph was showing mercy to Mary by seeking a quiet divorce and avoiding public scandal for her.

Summary: Jesus is a child of the nation of Israel. His ancestors were sinners but also people who remembered the promise of God: that Israel would be a blessing to everyone on earth. Jesus was born to Mary and Joseph to be the Promise of God and God's salvation for all on earth.

Help students reflect: Do you need a savior? What needs to be saved in your life? How can God help to save you from your sins? Jesus's family tree includes murderers, adulterers, prostitutes, and liars. Why do you think God chose to be born to this family? Why associate himself with these people? Mary is found with child through the Holy Spirit. What does the Spirit do?

The Light Shines in the Darkness

Christmas Day
John 1:1-18

Background information:
The Word is Jesus, who is God, who created the universe and everything in it. John is the last of the prophets who foretold the coming of Jesus into the world. The reading is strange; think of it like an ancient poem describing the creation of the world and Jesus as the Word and the Creator.

Summary: The God of the world has come into the world which He created. He entered into the world in an event called the *Incarnation*, in which he took on a human life. Jesus is the incarnation of God, who came to live with us and to give thanks for us and with us to God. Jesus was outside of the world He created, but then entered it in order to save us from our sins. He did not need the world but chose to come into its darkness in order to save it for our sake.

Help students reflect:
God became a human person not in the life of a billionaire, not as the president of a nation, not even an influencer: not powerful, not rich, not honorable, but normal. Jesus was born poor, an immigrant, far from family and friends. He moved from one country to another when He was a kid and even some of his family had trouble accepting Him. He grew up, had chores at home, had a curfew, had friends, played games, prayed and went to school. He was normal. He was also God. Can you trust a God like that? What would you talk to Him about?

The Birth of Jesus

How does the birth of Jesus fulfill God's promise to His people?

→ long-expected MESSIAH

Why do you think that Matthew felt it was so important to track and document the full list of Jesus's ancestors? What does this list show us?

→ The blessing of a Messiah promised to us in the Old Testament was to be a descendant of David. The lineage shows that David was Jesus's ancestor.

Somewhere in the image below, use creative lettering to sketch out a key word, phrase, or quote of your choice from this Gospel.

What is most surprising to you about the way that God sent Jesus into the world? Inside the boxes, use sketches or creative lettering to give 3 details about Jesus's birth that are unexpected. Then color as you reflect on the bigger picture. What is most incredible about God's plan here?

"God is with us"

He will Save His people from their sins

Weak / not strong

Poor & humble

young / can't talk

Matthew 1:1-25

Teacher Notes: Gospel Doodle Reflections — Cycle Year "C"

The Boy Jesus in the Temple

Feast of the Holy Family
Luke 2:41-52

Background information:
- This is the only story about Jesus's youth in the Bible. It portrays Him as being a faithful and obedient Jewish boy, raised in the religious traditions of Israel, and fulfilling Jewish law.[3]
- Luke's gospel begins the story of Jesus's birth with Zechariah and Elizabeth in the temple. Now Luke ends the story of Jesus's childhood with another temple story.
- Twelve years old was the age of the time to accept religious responsibility in Judaism. Luke tells this story as a transition from Jesus's infancy to adult ministry.

Summary: The Holy Family travels in caravan to Jerusalem to celebrate one of the great holy days of Judaism: Passover. While there, pre-teen Jesus cuts from His family. Mary and Joseph realize they lost Jesus and return distraught to find Jesus in the temple. Jesus does not seem to understand His parents' emotions but shows His maturity and commitment to God in other ways.

Help students reflect: Two main themes here are maturing to adulthood and relationship with parents. How do people begin to take adult responsibility in Christianity? Have you seen yourself interested in any of these things? Why did Jesus not understand His parents? What is challenging about seeing things from your parents' viewpoint? How does Jesus know God is His Father?

The Epiphany of the Lord
Matthew 2:1-12

Background information:
- King Herod in this story is the uncle of the King Herod who will be involved in Jesus's crucifixion. Both King Herods are appointed "King of the Jews" by the Roman Emperor.
- Magi were likely astrologers: the scientists of the day. They accept Jesus before the Jews.[4]
- Herod is seeking out Jesus the way Pharoah sought out the child Moses, in order to eliminate Him (compare Matthew Ch. 2 to Exodus Ch. 1). The good will of the Magi, who do not return to Herod, ultimately saves Jesus's life.
- The Bible does not call the Magi "kings." The interpretation of these Old Testament passages led to this name: Psalm 72:10, Isaiah 60:6.[5]

Summary: King Herod learns of the birth of a competing King of the Jews (Jesus) and uses the Magi in a nefarious plan to destroy Jesus. The Magi find Jesus, worship Him, offer Him kingly gifts, and depart to protect Jesus's safety, foiling the plan of Herod.

Help students reflect:
King Herod couldn't respect Jesus's life. Can you think of any lives that are not respected today? How do we show respect for the lives of others? The Epiphany is a celebration of Jesus "appearing" to the world. How does Jesus appear in the world today? How does His message about God being our loving Father reach people?

ORDINARY TIME

Teacher Notes: Gospel Doodle Reflections　　　　　　　　　　　　　　　　　**Cycle Year "C"**

You Are My Beloved Son

ORDINARY TIME

The Baptism of Jesus
Luke 3:15-16, 21-22

Background information:
- The time of John the Baptist's ministry has been called "The Time of the Promise." The time of Jesus's ministry is called "The Time of Fulfillment." The next story about Jesus is the temptation in the desert, so Luke is using The Baptism as a transition to Jesus's ministry.[6]
- It was true that people were filled with expectation: the Jews longed for release from their subordination to the Roman empire. The Jews longed for the promised Messiah of the Old Testament who would free them of their captors.
- John the Baptist is called "the forerunner" because he prepared people for Jesus. Jesus and John are cousins (Elizabeth, John's mom, is Mary's cousin).

Summary: The people are seeing John the Baptist live an incredible life of austerity and preach in a way that some began to think John was the Messiah. John corrects this error, Jesus is baptized, and the heavens open up to announce that Jesus is the Son of God.

Help students reflect: Because Jesus is God, Jesus being baptized by John is like a student baptizing the principal of the school. Why would Jesus be so humble? What does this act of humility say about the way Jesus views John? How can we grow to be humble this way? (See next page to help students renew their Baptismal promises.)

The Wedding at Cana

The Second Sunday of Ordinary Time
John 2:1-11

Background information:
- Jesus's "hour" refers to His time of passion, death, resurrection, and ascension.
- The "headwaiter" would have been a kind of "emcee," probably a relative of the family.
- This is the first of seven "signs" that Jesus performs according to John's gospel (John is also the only one to call them "signs" instead of "miracles.")

Summary: Jesus and His disciples attend a wedding. When the wine runs out, Jesus's mother, Mary, demands that Jesus help save the newlyweds from the embarrassment of running out of wine. Jesus does not want to perform the miracle but obeys his mom. The party can continue with everyone amazed that the best has been saved for last.

Help students reflect: This whole story is trying to teach us that even when we run out of the things we think are good, Jesus gives us what is truly good. He literally gives us the "good wine" in His precious blood at Mass, but in **everything** Jesus gives us what is truly good. What sorts of things does Jesus give us? Why does He sometimes wait to give us things until we've run out of the good things in our lives? What are some obstacles to our faith in the fact that He is always taking care of us? How can the "good wine" at the Wedding at Cana be a symbol for God the Father's love for each of us?

Renewal of Baptismal Promises

Teacher / Parent reads each, pausing after each question. Students respond "I do" to each.

(3 to REJECT):

Do you reject Satan?

I do.

And all his works?

I do.

And all his empty promises?

I do.

(3 to AFFIRM):

Do you believe in God, the Father Almighty, creator of heaven and earth?

I do.

Do you believe in Jesus Christ, his only Son, our Lord, who was born of the Virgin Mary, was crucified, died, and was buried, rose from the dead, and is now seated at the right hand of the Father?

I do.

Do you believe in the Holy Spirit, the holy Catholic church, the communion of saints, the forgiveness of sins, the resurrection of the body, and life everlasting?

I do.

(Final Blessing):

God, the all-powerful Father of our Lord Jesus Christ has given us a new birth by water and the Holy Spirit, and forgiven all our sins. May he also keep us faithful to our Lord Jesus Christ for ever and ever.

Amen.

SAMPLE

You Are My Beloved Son

Luke 3:15-16, 21-22

At our own Baptisms, we also are identified as God's beloved sons and daughters. Do a renewal of your baptismal vows here by writing the three rejections and three affirmations of belief that we usually do when we renew our Baptismal promises.

reject

1 Satan

2 his works

3 his empty promises

affirm

1 creator FATHER

2 SON (died + rose)

3 HOLY SPIRIT, Catholic church, forgiveness, eternal life...

Renew Baptismal promises

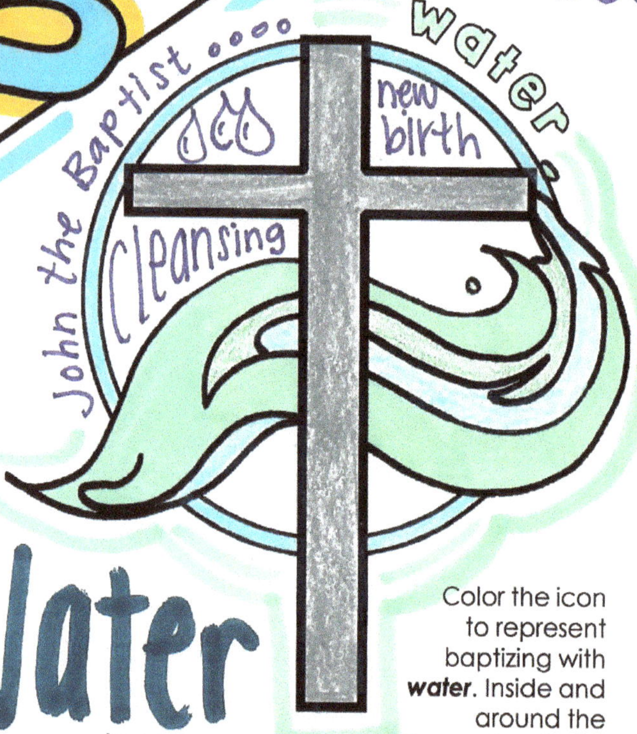

John the Baptist
water
new birth
cleansing

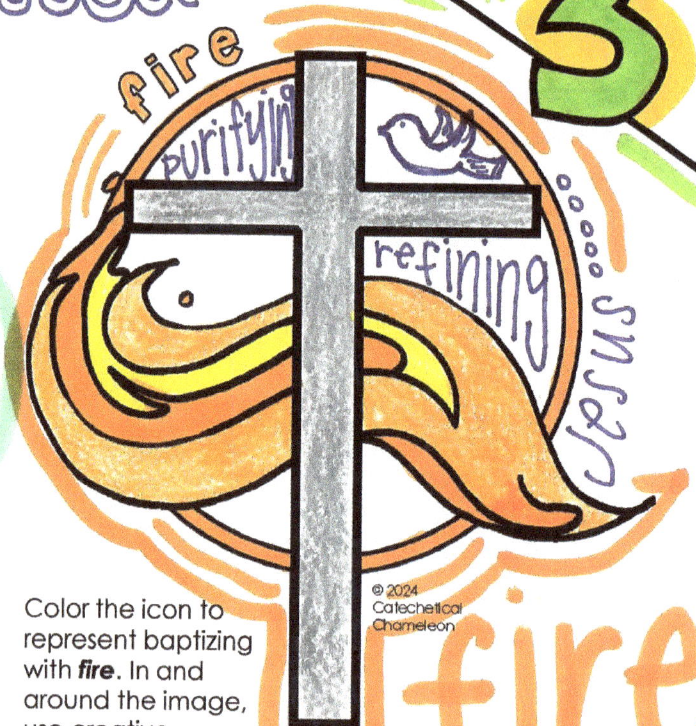

fire
purifying
refining
Jesus

Water

Color the icon to represent baptizing with ***water***. Inside and around the image, use creative lettering or doodles to represent who baptized with water, and what this type of Baptism is all about.

fire

Color the icon to represent baptizing with ***fire***. In and around the image, use creative lettering or doodles to represent who would baptize with fire and the Holy Spirit, and what this type of Baptism is all about.

When Jesus prayed, the heavens opened. When we pray, God & the heavens are opened to us as well. As you color, reflect on this Gospel and pray about it.

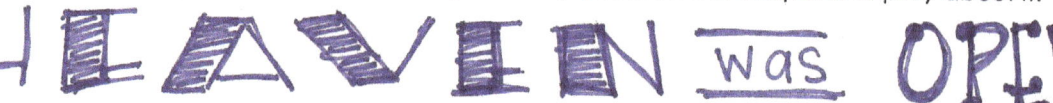

"HEAVEN was OPENED"

Teacher Notes: Gospel Doodle Reflections **Cycle Year "C"**

Ministry in Galilee

The Third Sunday of Ordinary Time
Luke 1:1-4, 4:14-21

Background information:
- Luke addresses his Gospel to Theophilus: "Lover of God"
- This could be a specific person, but it also could be meant as a reference to every Christian
- In this Gospel Jesus has returned to Nazareth to follow the Jewish rules and attend the Synagogue where Jews worshiped God and prayed.

Summary: Luke explains to the audience that he is going to write down the full story of Jesus so that everyone can read and know what really happened. Jesus is returning to Galilee, and is teaching people about God. He goes to His Hometown of Nazareth. In the synagogue, Jesus reads aloud from the Scroll of Isaiah. In the part Jesus reads, Isaiah is saying that he had come to bring the good news and proclaim the release of prisoners. When He finishes reading Jesus says: "Today this Scripture has been fulfilled in your hearing." He says this because He, (Jesus) is the Good News and He will free people from their sins.

Help students reflect: Jesus is an example of how to Love God by reading the Bible and going to church every week. When is the last time you read your Bible? How can you find time to learn about Jesus every week?

Jesus in Nazareth

The Fourth Sunday of Ordinary Time
Luke 4:21-30

Background information:
Jesus is in His Hometown of Nazareth and just read from the Prophet Isaiah and said that He was the Fulfillment of Isaiah's promises.

Summary: The People listened to Jesus and His teachings, but they were surprised that He claimed to be the Good News and would free the prisoners because they knew that He was the son of Joseph the carpenter. The crowd wants Jesus to perform miracles for them, to prove that He is who He said He was, but Jesus says that they won't accept Him because this is His home, and they just believe that He is Joseph's son. They don't believe that He could be something more, so they get angry with Him.

Help students reflect: The people in Nazareth couldn't believe that Jesus was anything but a simple carpenter. Are there times when you are angry with Jesus because He won't do or say what you want? What have you done today to show that you believe in Jesus?

ORDINARY TIME

Teacher Notes: Gospel Doodle Reflections **Cycle Year "C"**

Do Not Be Afraid

The Fifth Sunday of Ordinary Time
Luke 5:1-11

Background information:
- Jesus was recognized as "a teacher." In ancient Judaism, men like Jesus would travel around giving lessons, sometimes impromptu: this appears to be the case when Jesus asks to borrow Simon's boat.
- Simon, James, and John were fishermen. They left their livelihood to follow Jesus. Following teachers was an exciting and promising way of life in that time.

Summary: Jesus teaches the crowds on Lake Gennesaret from Simon's boat. Afterwards, Jesus encourages Simon to go fishing once more. Simon catches too many fish and recognizes that Jesus is more than just another rabbi. He truly knows God. Simon, James, and John agree to follow Jesus and become the first disciples (Mark's gospel includes Andrew as well).

Help students reflect: Where do you need a lot of a good thing in your life? In grades? With friends? In sports? Getting chores done? Do you trust Jesus to help you make a big catch? If Jesus can help you with these things, what else can you trust Him with?

The Beatitudes

The Sixth Sunday of Ordinary Time
Luke 6:17, 20-26

Background information:
- "Beatitude" comes from the Latin word "beatus," meaning "blessed."
- The missing verses 18 and 19 contain healing and exorcism stories which would be difficult to explain to modern ears in a homily.
- Luke's beatitudes are meant to be contrasted with Matthew 5:1-12. Matthew is more spiritual while Luke is more practical.[7]

Summary: Jesus takes to a plain with a large crowd following Him. There He begins teaching and of first order are the beatitudes and woes. Here, Jesus shares his gospel project for transforming our perspective on wealth.

Help students reflect: Is it special to be rich, popular, or well-off? Might there be anything more important in life? What about family, friendship, or simply caring about others? Here, Jesus flips our perspectives upside down: it is really the rich who are pitiable, those with good food who need our assistance, those who are happy who need to be consoled, the popular who need true friendship. Why is this the case? Perhaps, all these things are too shallow: the result of luck, but not necessarily true love. After all, Jesus died poor, hungry, unpopular, and grieving on a cross. But He had love. And the poor people have Him. Do we?

ORDINARY TIME

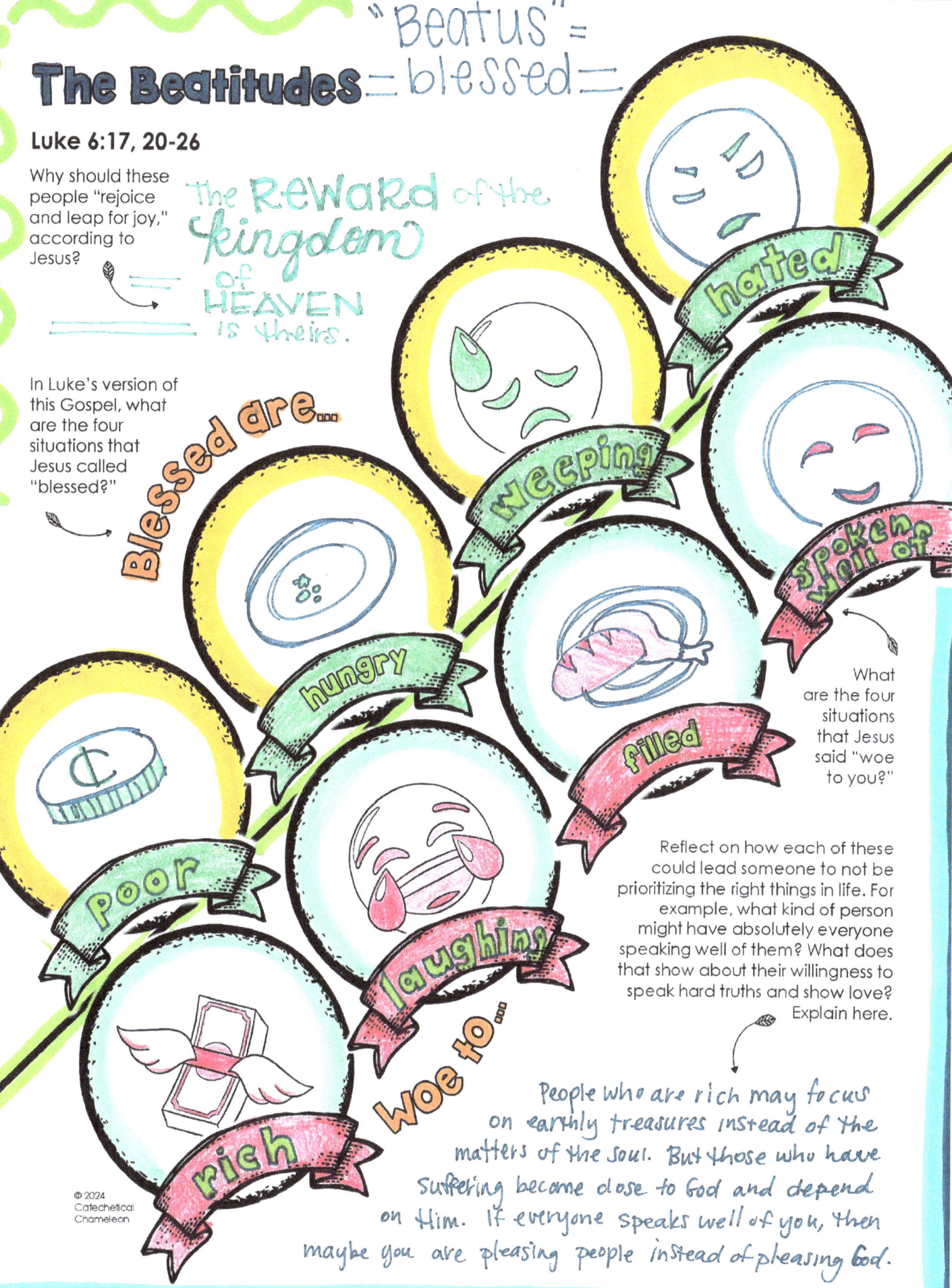

Teacher Notes: Gospel Doodle Reflections   Cycle Year "C"

Be Merciful

The Seventh Sunday of Ordinary Time
Luke 6:27-38

Background information:
- Luke's "Sermon on the Plain" is a part of Jesus's ministry in Galilee. It contains Luke's Beatitudes and four main teachings (love your enemies, judging others, tree known by its fruit, and two foundations). Today, we get the first two teachings.
- In the Old Testament, it was expected that Israelites would love their neighbors and love some foreigners as well, but certainly not their *enemies*. Jesus broadens the law of love to encompass everyone without distinction.

Summary: Jesus gives two teachings to a large crowd, of which he had just healed many (v.18). In order to be children of the Most High, we have to love our enemies, our persecutors, and those who steal from us. That is *mercy*. The second teaching is like it: don't judge or condemn others, but forgive and we will be forgiven.

Help students reflect: Who might it be difficult for us to love today? Who are our enemies? Do we love them? Why is it so difficult? Why is it so important to love everyone?
When Jesus asks us to stop judging, does that mean we can't know right from wrong?

The Splinter in the Eye

The Eighth Sunday of Ordinary Time
Luke 6:39-45

Background information:
- This Gospel continues Jesus's teaching on judgment from last week and adds the teaching of good and rotten fruit.
- There is a great artwork portraying Jesus's 'splinter in the eye' teaching. Try an internet search: "the mote and the beam."
- Jesus's teaching on judgment was meant to be read together with the teaching on good and rotten fruit.

Summary: Jesus continues the Sermon on the Plain with a fuller teaching on judging others and His teaching on good and rotten fruit. He reminds us that good and evil fruit arises from the character of a person's heart. Lastly, Jesus reminds us that we can tell a lot about a person just from the way they talk.

Help students reflect: Can we think of a time where we saw a tiny splinter in someone else's eye, but we couldn't see the huge beam in our own eye? Are there any stories that could be shared? Pause and think for a minute if there might be a situation like that right now.
Who is someone in our life that bears good fruit? What makes them so good?

Teacher Notes: Gospel Doodle Reflections   **Cycle Year "C"**

Only Say the Word

The Ninth Sunday of Ordinary Time
Luke 7:1-10

Background information:
- The Sermon on the Plain has ended, and now Jesus is on the move again.
- A centurion was a Roman Military Officer, like a "Captain" in the US Army today.
- It was considered 'unclean' for a Jew to go into the house of a gentile.
- It is from this Gospel that our response at the Lamb of God during Mass is taken: "Lord I am not worthy that you should enter under my roof, but only say the word and my soul shall be healed."

Summary: Jesus enters Capernaum and finds a roman centurion with an ill servant. Though the roman is not a Jew, Jesus gives the healing anyway (in faithfulness to His teachings on love and judgment just a moment before). Jesus praises the roman's faith and heals the servant.

Help students reflect: Is there anyone that we are not supposed to like? A rival school or sports team? A difficult classmate? What can we do to love that person/people? How about the words, "I am not worthy to have you enter under my roof." Why is that easy or difficult to understand? Why doesn't Jesus care if we are "worthy" or not?

The Tenth Sunday of Ordinary Time
Luke 7:11-17

Background information:
- There are no better proofs of Jesus's true humanity than these passages of His grief and compassion.
- One of the reasons the Pharisees hated Jesus is because He was famous for raising the dead. Jesus would have known this. He would not have wanted to make enemies with them, but He cannot resist helping people.
- This passage is meant to remind us of Elijah's raising of a widow's son: 1 Kings 7:8-24.

Summary: After healing the centurion's servant, Jesus sees a widow in grief for the death of her only son. Can there be a greater loneliness? Jesus raises the young man from the dead and gives him back to his mother. All are shocked and the story spreads everywhere.

Help students reflect:
Who do you know who has compassion like Jesus? Think of friends, your mother or father, your grandparents, and your teachers. Does Jesus's love and compassion remind you of anyone? Why does Jesus say, "Do not weep?" Does He ever talk to you this way? How do you think that Jesus cares about you? What does it mean that Jesus has authority even over death? How is it possible that He can raise people from the dead? What does this mean for your life?

ORDINARY TIME

Teacher Notes: Gospel Doodle Reflections   Cycle Year "C"

Your Sins Are Forgiven

The Eleventh Sunday of Ordinary Time
Luke 7:36-8:3

Background information:
- The fact that Jesus dined at a Pharisee's home is notable because Jesus did not dine only with the poor, but with the rich and important also.
- The difference between the Pharisee and the sinful woman is this - One accepted forgiveness and love. The other did not.
- Theologically, Jesus suggests that to love is to be forgiven.

Summary: Jesus goes to dinner at the house of a Pharisee (a religious leader and ruler). While there, He receives unexceptional treatment by the Pharisee, but unique and loving treatment by a woman who was known to be a sinner. To this woman, Jesus gives forgiveness of sins. Afterward, Jesus continues His journey proclaiming the Kingdom of God amidst the Twelve and many women.

Help students reflect: Sometimes, everyone important writes us off. Do we see ourselves as forgiven by Christ? The sinful woman shows great love towards Jesus. Do we realize that if we love Jesus, all can be forgiven? Is there anyone today that we are called to forgive?

Who Do You Say that I Am?

The Twelfth Sunday of Ordinary Time
Luke 9:18-24

Background information:
- The disciples often wondered who Jesus was. How could they not, with all the miracles? Here, Jesus asks them directly about His identity.
- Jesus was often compared to John the Baptist because of His radical teachings.
- To most Jews, 'Christ' or Messiah meant a political savior, who would free Israel from Roman control and reestablish the Israeli nation as King. This idea is what Jesus warns against in v. 21.

Summary: After praying in solitude, Jesus suddenly asked His disciples what people thought His identity was. The disciples gave several good Jewish answers and then Peter spoke up and said "the Christ:" meaning, the savior and new king of Israel. Jesus rebuked them and corrected them saying that the Christ was not a political savior but must suffer and die.

Help students reflect:
Who are our saviors, heroes, or idols who we think will lead us to some kind of promised land? Jesus knew that He was not a political savior. Does this shake our confidence in politicians? Jesus knew that the savior of the world would suffer greatly. Why would this be the case? Why would the world not accept a suffering savior? Why is it important to give our lives back to God if we are going to keep them? Why is sacrifice a prerequisite for success?

ORDINARY TIME

Teacher Notes: Gospel Doodle Reflections   **Cycle Year "C"**

I Will Follow Wherever You Go

ORDINARY TIME

The Thirteenth Sunday of Ordinary Time
Luke 9:51-62

Background information:
- Starting here, Jesus begins His journey to Jerusalem.
- It is worth noting that the Samaritans reject Jesus here. Samaritans and Jews were like mortal enemies in Jesus's day. Jesus loved both, and both hated Him.

Summary: Jesus continues along the way to Jerusalem and enters a Samaritan village. He is rejected there and His disciples, feeling the offense, ask Him to smite the village. Jesus rebukes them and continues to teach. A Christian's true homeland is Heaven. Earthly things are passing.

Help students reflect: Who has rejected you? Who do you wish you could get back at? Who gets you angry and competitive? Do you ever feel like the disciples, wanting to call down fire from the sky to eliminate these people? Why does Jesus rebuke/reject this attitude? Jesus says that disciples have no true place to rest. What does this mean? Could it mean that the mission is too important to rest? Is Jesus more important than family? Is Christianity more important than family? Is this the most difficult teaching of Christianity?

Peace to this Household

The Fourteenth Sunday of Ordinary Time
Luke 10:1-12, 17-20

Background information:
- Here, Jesus continues on His way from Galilee to Jerusalem, preparing for His Passion.
- The mission Jesus gives His disciples is so important that even money and polite greetings are a waste of time.
- "I See Satan Fall Like Lightning" is the title of a book by a famous anthropologist and humanist of the 20th century: Rene Girard.

Summary: Jesus sends representatives into the towns to witness to Him, then He speaks about the difficulty of finding good ministers. He instructs the 72: carry no possessions. Proclaim peace to every household. Do not waste your time with people who do not welcome you. Proclaim that the Kingdom is at hand.

Help students reflect: Why is being a disciple so demanding? Why do we need to forget every worldly possession and even put Jesus before our families? What makes Jesus so great? Why is 'peace' the most important thing to give to people we are evangelizing? Why do we need to know when to move on in life (shake the dust off our sandals)? What does it mean that Jesus says, "I have seen Satan fall like lightning?"

Teacher Notes: Gospel Doodle Reflections   Cycle Year "C"

The Good Samaritan

The Fifteenth Sunday of Ordinary Time
Luke 10:25-37

Background information:
- The scholars of the law were members of the religious elite, who tied up heavy burdens for people, but without loving them.
- Jesus was constantly harassed by the religious authorities who put law above love.
- The priest and Levite in the parable are the ones that would have been expected to be models of charity: instead, they are preoccupied with rules. Samaritans, on the other hand, were enemies of the Jewish people, so the story is a bit surprising.

Summary: Jesus is tested by a scholar of the law regarding entrance to eternal life. The scholar knows the correct answer but does not have the love to live it out freely. Jesus shares the parable of the Good Samaritan to show what He means by true love.

Help students reflect: Have you ever been in a situation where it was hard to love someone because life was too busy or because you had something else you felt was more important? Has anyone ever surprised you by caring about you when you were feeling down? What kind of groups of people are difficult to love?

Martha & Mary

The Sixteenth Sunday of Ordinary Time
Luke 10:38-42

Background information:
- Martha and Mary were friends of Jesus, together with their brother Lazarus.
- Much like today, in ancient Israel, if you welcomed a guest into your home, you were expected to provide food and water to excess.

Summary: Martha and Mary welcome Jesus into their home. Mary sits at Jesus's feet and listens to Him while Martha runs around doing what she thinks is essential. Jesus tells her not to worry about what everyone else thinks she should do and just enjoy the company.

Help students reflect: Do you ever have too much going on and it is difficult to really enjoy time with people? What is that experience like? Why is there so much pressure to "get things done?" Is it ok to let go of the checklist in order to spend time with God or with the people we love? Why are we afraid sometimes to let go of the way we think things are supposed to be in order to spend quality time with people? Why is quality time with others better than getting things done?

ORDINARY TIME

Teacher Notes: Gospel Doodle Reflections　　　　　　　　　　**Cycle Year "C"**

The Lord's Prayer

The Seventeenth Sunday of Ordinary Time
Luke 11:1-13

Background information:
- A fuller "Our Father" prayer is found in the Gospel of Matthew (Matthew 6:9-13).
- The "Our Father" prayer has been used at Christian celebrations from the earliest times. It is truly an ancient prayer.

Summary: Jesus teaches His disciples to pray and instructs them specifically how to do it. God is not distant. He is not bothered. He does not give anyone anything bad. God loves us and cares for us as a Father. When you pray, think of yourself like a child asking your loving father who will give you whatever you need.

Help students reflect: Why might it be difficult to see God as a father?
When we see God as our father, how does that make us feel? How does that change what we might ask for in prayer? How does that impact out trust in the one we're praying to?

Parable of the Rich Fool

The Eighteenth Sunday of Ordinary Time
Luke 12:13-21

Background information:
- Jesus was not a rich man in His lifetime. Although He did have many disciples at different times, He lived very simply. At times, Jesus did not even have a place to sleep.
- Greed could be defined as the inordinate attachment to material things. It could also be defined as putting possessions ahead of people or ahead of God.

Summary: Jesus teaches His disciples a lesson on greed. A man approaches and asks for his share of inheritance. At face value, this is a simple matter of justice. He appeals to Jesus's authority as a teacher to get what is rightly his. Jesus distances himself from the situation and tells everyone not to concern themselves with treasures.

Help students reflect: It is possible to live in poverty in America and still be richer than half of the global population. Sometimes we don't realize just how well off we are. So, Jesus might say, why are we not happy? What do you think?
Why can't possessions make people perfectly happy?
Is it possible for a person who is rich in friendships and in God, but who is poor in the world to be happy? Why or why not?

ORDINARY TIME

Teacher Notes: Gospel Doodle Reflections　　　　　　　　　　　　**Cycle Year "C"**

Be Prepared

The Nineteenth Sunday of Ordinary Time
Luke 12:32-48

Background information:
Jesus uses His characteristic loving, comforting voice at the beginning of this gospel. Then, Jesus transitions to His (equally characteristic) sternness and high expectations for His disciples.

Summary: Jesus revisits His teaching from last week about riches before discussing the possibility of the end times (the coming of the Son of Man). He compares our waiting for this time to servants awaiting their master's return. Will we be ready when the master returns? Jesus says it will be better to be ignorant of the Master than to contradict Him.

Help students reflect: Jesus tells us, "do not be afraid any longer, little flock. The Father is pleased to give you the kingdom." How do these words make you feel?
Jesus follows those words up with much more challenging ones about being vigilant for our master's arrival. How do we balance the affection and love Jesus has for us with His difficult words about being ready? Can love be both caring **and** tough? Why?

I Have Come to Set Fire

The Twentieth Sunday of Ordinary Time
Luke 12:49-53

Background information:
- Jesus was a man of deep emotions, some of which are on display in this gospel.
- Jesus's words here stand in contrast to His name "Prince of Peace" (Isaiah 9:6) and to the appearance of angels to the shepherds (Luke 2:14). His words also are, in a way, obvious: not everyone accepts the gospel we preach.

Summary: Jesus preaches to His disciples that divisions will occur because of the gospel. Although it is a path of peace, still there will be conflict and disagreement.

Help students reflect: Jesus comes to set our lives on fire with enthusiasm for the gospel, the good news. Who do you know who has enthusiasm for the gospel? Have you ever seen anyone who was **on fire for Christ**? What would that life look like?
Jesus does not want us to become separated from our families. But, He does want us to believe that the gospel is of greater importance. Can we accept this? Why or why not?

ORDINARY TIME

Teacher Notes: Gospel Doodle Reflections — Cycle Year "C"

ORDINARY TIME

Strive

The Twenty-First Sunday of Ordinary Time
Luke 13:22-30

Background information:
- The Gospel is not a cuddly little Squishmallow. It is not designed only for comfort. Sometimes it also convicts, judges, and challenges. No one ever won a state championship by being told that they were good all the time. Sports legends were often their own worst critics.
- This gospel could be terrifying. Keep in mind a couple of other verses: Luke 1:37, Matthew 19:26, John 14:2-3.

Summary: As Jesus is journeying to Jerusalem, He is asked how many will be saved. Jesus answers that the gate is narrow, but we should strive to enter nonetheless.

Help students reflect: Do we think it will be easy to be saved? Or do we think that it will take hard work? If you think it will take hard work, what kind of work does it take? What do you have to do? Is there any of it that you already do? What do you think the next step is for yourself?
Even though Jesus is saying "strive" because it takes work, is it really our work that makes us saved, or is it God's work, or both? Why?

Humility & Exaltation

The Twenty-Second Sunday of Ordinary Time
Luke 14:1, 7-14

Background information:
- Jesus, as a rabbi by profession, would attend dinner with pharisees and scribes from time to time.
- Jesus, probably, would not have been given the seat of honor due to the dislike the pharisees had for Him.

Summary: Jesus attends dinner at the house of a pharisee, among other guests. While there, He gives two teachings: first, regarding places of honor and second, regarding who to invite when you hold a banquet. In both cases, Jesus teaches that we should take the humbler route.

Help students reflect: This is a good gospel for us to think about at school. When we sit down at lunch, do we try to sit next to the most popular students or do we humble ourselves and sit in another place, allowing ourselves to be called by others?
When we throw birthday parties or pick teams at recess, do we choose the humble kids first or do we immediately choose the best of the best?
Why might Jesus's way be an easier, kinder, and happier way to live?

Teacher Notes: Gospel Doodle Reflections — Cycle Year "C"

Discipleship

The Twenty-Third Sunday of Ordinary Time
Luke 14:25-33

Background information:
- Part of this teaching is also found in Matthew 10:37. Keep in mind the fourth commandment (Exodus 20:12) and other New Testament teachings (Ephesians 6:23).
- Jesus is not asking us, literally, to hate our parents. He is only using hyperbole to make us realize that the Gospel is an even greater good than family life.

Summary: Jesus continues His journey to Jerusalem and now great crowds are following Him (He is now famous for His miracles). He offers several teachings on discipleship. First, the subjection of family life to the gospel. Second, the need to carry our cross. Lastly, the need to plan ahead so as to live apart from our possessions.

Help students reflect: Which of the teachings here do you think is the most difficult? What cross are you called to carry in your life right now? Is anyone helping you to carry it? What possessions could you detach from? How could you give those things to God instead of holding on tight to them?

Parables

The Twenty-Fourth Sunday of Ordinary Time
Luke 15:1-32

Background information:
- After several weeks of difficult and challenging gospels, we get three of the most merciful parables right in a row. This Sunday feels like a deep breath.
- A parable is a story with an example that teaches a lesson.
- In Jesus's time, society was a bit more divided into "good people" and "bad people." "Sinners" were people who committed adultery, or financial crime, or other public mistakes and they were treated as a group of outcasts. Jesus took a lot of criticism because He treated them like human beings.
- The parables all use irony or extreme examples: who would expect someone to leave 99 sheep behind, or invite their friends over because they found one coin, or easily forgive the son who treated you as dead?

Summary: Jesus preaches to Pharisees, tax collectors, and sinners with these three awesome parables - The Parable of the Lost Sheep, the Parable of the Lost Coin, and the Parable of the Prodigal Son. Each time the message is that God prioritizes sinners. God values what the world sees as being of little or no value.

Help students reflect: Are we ever tempted to treat others like outcasts or sinners? Have we ever felt treated that way? Is it weird that God values what the world does not value? How does this challenge our notions of who is important in the world?

Teacher Notes: Gospel Doodle Reflections **Cycle Year "C"**

The Dishonest Steward

The Twenty-Fifth Sunday of Ordinary Time
Luke 16:1-13

Background information:
- There is a valuable explanation of this parable which can be found in the notes of the New American Bible Revised Edition. In sum, the dishonest steward removed the 10% he would ordinarily have taken off the top of those transactions in order to make himself appreciated among his master's debtors.[8]
- Jesus is not teaching dishonesty here, but prudence.

Summary: Jesus teaches His disciples that they are to be wise in the ways of the world. He offers as an example a steward who squandered his master's property and was about to be fired. What could he do, except try to make friends with as many people as he could while he had time? Maybe one of them would later have a job for him. The basic teaching here is trustworthiness. If corrupt people can trust you, how much more the incorrupt?

Help students reflect: This parable could be a difficult one to apply to our own lives. But consider this - maybe you're not the best student, but you're always kind to the teacher. On the day of the exam, your teacher is more likely to give you bonus points, right? Learn to be wise, and if you can, it will be a service to the church and to the Gospel.

The Rich Man and Lazarus

The Twenty-Sixth Sunday of Ordinary Time
Luke 16:19-31

Background information:
- Of the four gospels, Luke's gospel is most concerned with Jesus's attitude towards the poor.
- This gospel is meant to illustrate Jesus's teaching in the Sermon on the Mount: "blessed are the poor."

Summary: A rich man lives his life of enjoyment while outside, Lazarus suffers from poverty, sickness and abuse, even from dogs. The rich man never shares any of his wealth with Lazarus, although later the rich man shows he knows Lazarus's name. Both men die and Lazarus goes to Heaven while the rich man goes to Hell. There is a chasm that prevents Lazarus from helping the rich man in Hell and Abraham tells the rich man that not even the resurrection of the dead can convince rich people to convert from their selfish ways.

Help students reflect: What kinds of poverty are there? There is poverty of money and possessions, but also of friendship, mercy, smarts, achievement and many more. Even pride is a kind of weakness, a poverty: people with ego are poor in humility. Quietly think about who you know that is poor in some way. Do you ignore that person or do you go out of your way to help them, to recognize and appreciate them? What prevents you from going out of your way to help others?

ORDINARY TIME

Teacher Notes: Gospel Doodle Reflections **Cycle Year "C"**

ORDINARY TIME

Faith to Move Mountains

The Twenty-Seventh Sunday of Ordinary Time
Luke 17:5-10

Background information:
- The request of the disciples comes after the story of Lazarus and the rich man. We can understand why the disciples may have been nervous about their level of faith after a story like that!

Summary: After the story of Lazarus, the disciples request that Jesus increase their faith. Jesus replies with His teaching of the mustard seed followed by the teaching on being a servant. Jesus's point is to say that the Christian shouldn't consider himself or herself special because of his or her faith, but acknowledge that the faith is exactly how life should be lived anyway.

Help students reflect: Where do we expect special treatment in life? When our dad is our coach? When we have done all our chores without complaining? When we got our homework in on time or cleaned up after ourselves?
What is the benefit of doing what we are expected to do if there is no special reward for it?
What are some other ways we can do as we are expected?
Who are good examples of people that do what they are supposed to do without looking for any extra reward?

The Cleansing of Lepers

The Twenty-Eighth Sunday of Ordinary Time
Luke 17:11-19

Background information:
Lepers existed on the outskirts of villages, far enough away that the villagers would not worry that they would also contract the disease.
Samaritans were enemies of the Jews. Jesus makes the point again that the Gospel is not limited to the "in" crowd. He is here for everyone who will follow.

Summary: Jesus continues to approach Jerusalem and this time encounters lepers on the outskirts of a town. They recognize Him as a healer and beg Him for healing, but after they are healed only one returns to thank Jesus. To this one, Jesus gives salvation.

Help students reflect: There are all sorts of things we would like to be healed from, even if we're not lepers. We want better grades, better athleticism, more popularity, better mental health. All of this is a kind of healing we seek. Do we ask Jesus for these things? What does He say to us?
Do we recognize that healing is not as important as salvation? 10 lepers were healed, but only one was saved. What can we do to put faith before our desire for healing? What can we do to seek salvation first?

Teacher Notes: Gospel Doodle Reflections   **Cycle Year "C"**

Prayer of the Persistent Widow

The Twenty-Ninth Sunday of Ordinary Time
Luke 18:1-8

Background information:
This parable and the one next Sunday come at the end of Jesus's teaching ministry prior to His encounter with Zaccheus and His entrance into Jerusalem.

Summary: Jesus gives this teaching about persistence in prayer. The judge neither fears God nor man, but when a widow comes to him day after day begging for a just decision, he realizes it would be better to give her what she wants. Jesus says, will not God, who is good, bring justice more quickly to his chosen people than a godless human?

Help students reflect: Do we ever get discouraged in prayer? Do we ever wonder if God is even listening? Maybe God hears your prayer, but wants to see you trust Him even more or give even more of your confidence and faith over to Him.
In any case, the most important result of prayer is our increased trust in God. He will never fail you. You can count on Him.
What are you praying for right now? How might you pray more persistently?

Pharisee vs. Tax Collector

The Thirtieth Sunday of Ordinary Time
Luke 18:9-14

Background information:
Jesus dealt with a lot of self-righteous Pharisees.

Summary: Jesus offers His second teaching on prayer. This time, telling the story of a proud Pharisee and a humble tax-collector, Jesus surprises everyone by saying that it is the humble sinner, and not the religious expert, who makes a prayer acceptable to God.

Help students reflect: Why might it be such a temptation for religious leaders to become self-righteous? Does this parable help us to understand why it is so important to pray for our priests and bishops?
Why does God prefer the prayer of the humble? And why do those who are humbled eventually get exalted?
Who do you know who is particularly humble? And what can you do during this phase of your own life to stay humble?

ORDINARY TIME

Teacher Notes: Gospel Doodle Reflections
Cycle Year "C"

Zacchaeus

The Thirty-First Sunday of Ordinary Time
Luke 19:1-10

Background information:
- Jericho is a city East of Jerusalem near the Dead Sea and the Jordan River.
- Jews who became tax collectors were among the least appreciated people in Jewish society: they were traitors who helped the Roman government extort Jews. Since Zacchaeus is a chief tax collector, he is particularly rich and unliked.

Summary: Jesus enters Jericho and crowds gather to see the miracle worker. Zacchaeus, who is nearing a conversion moment, is among them. Because he is short, he climbs a tree and there, Jesus sees him and calls him by name. The crowds grumble that such a sinner is receiving so much of Jesus's attention, but Zacchaeus truly converts and promises more than half of his wealth to the poor and those who deserve it.

Help students reflect: Who is undeserving of Jesus's time or attention? What is the conversion that Jesus is looking for that is available to people whether they are rich or poor? Why was it important that Zacchaeus was willing to give away so much of his wealth? What can you do to be more generous? Do you find the comment "He has gone to stay at the house of a sinner" ridiculous, given that we are **all** sinners? Who do you judge as a more obvious sinner because it is more clear that they are sinful than yourself, with your own less visible sins?

Question About the Resurrection

The Thirty-Second Sunday of Ordinary Time
Luke 20:27-38

Background information:
- Sadducees were another group of Jews with religious power in Jesus's time, like the Pharisees.
- Jesus seemed to have fewer documented run-ins with Sadducees, however.

Summary: The Sadducees came with a difficult question for Jesus since they did not believe in the Resurrection and Jesus did. Jesus responds that in eternal life there will not be a marriage.

Help students reflect: What is marriage for? Why is it so important to humanity and the human race? Why would marriage not need to exist in Heaven?
What does it mean to you to be like an angel, a child of God, one who will rise? What does it mean that to God, all are alive?

ORDINARY TIME

Teacher Notes: Gospel Doodle Reflections   Cycle Year "C"

The End of Days

The Thirty-Third Sunday of Ordinary Time
Luke 21:5-19

Background information:
The earliest Christians thought that the end times would arrive soon after Jesus's Ascension. As years went by they learned a more spiritual meaning to Jesus's words.

Summary: Jesus cautions His disciples about the end of days. It will be a great upheaval, with wars, earthquakes, and persecutions to spare. But as for the disciples, they should be patient and at peace, without even worrying about their own martyrdom. Finally, He reminds us that perseverance will win the day. Even if we never experience the "end of days" in our lifetime, Jesus's words apply equally well to the struggle we can prepare for in our final hours of life.

Help students reflect: Where in your life could you use a bit more perseverance? Who encourages you to persevere and remain strong? What kinds of thoughts take your peace away or make it difficult to persevere? Do you believe in life after death? Who helps you to feel secure and at peace about it? What does a belief in Jesus add to your wondering? Remember, the sufferings of the present time are nothing compared to the glory to be revealed to us.

Our Lord Jesus Christ, King of the Universe

The Final Sunday of Ordinary Time
Luke 23:35-43

Background information:
- This feast was instituted by Pope Pius XI in 1925 to reinvigorate devotion to the Roman Catholic Church and to Jesus Christ.
- Vatican II and Pope Paul VI brought this feast to new importance by making it equal to the greatest celebrations of the church and moving its celebration from October to the last Sunday of the liturgical year.
- In the gospel, the justification for Jesus's crucifixion is that He called Himself "the King of the Jews," and so set himself as a competitor to the Roman Emperor, Tiberius Caesar.
- St. Dismas is the good thief whom Jesus himself welcomed into paradise: this was probably the easiest canonization ever.

Summary: As Jesus dies on the cross for a crime He did not commit, He is mocked even by a criminal crucified alongside Him. The other criminal, a thief, rebukes the first criminal. He admits his guilt, accepts his punishment, and he professes Christ's innocence. He asks Jesus to remember him and Jesus responds, "You will be with me in Paradise."

Help students reflect: Is it strange that a criminal was one of the only people standing up for Jesus in His last hour? How does that contribute to your understanding of Jesus's mercy? How important is it to stand up against bullying? And why is Jesus always on the side of those being bullied? What does Jesus give us if we are the ones who stand up to bullying?

LENT

Teacher Notes: Gospel Doodle Reflections   **Cycle Year "C"**

Your Father Who Sees You

Ash Wednesday
Matthew 6:1-6, 16-18

Background information:
- Lent is a Latin word that means "springtime." Lent is all about new growth!
- The ashes used on Ash Wednesday come from the burning of the palm branches from the previous year's Palm Sunday.
- Did you know that a lot of current diets recommend "intermittent fasting" where only one meal is eaten a couple days every week?
- When Jesus talks about "hypocrites," He's referring to the Pharisees.

Summary: Here, Jesus teaches us to fast, give alms, and pray as a three-fold path to Christian holiness. He also teaches us to do all of these three in a spirit of humility, not to serve ourselves with attention. Finally, He reminds us that our Father always gives us His attention and is proud of the good things we do.

Help students reflect: Is Lent just about making our lives more difficult, or is there something else to it? What is the value of silence and being free from distractions in prayer? What is the value of taking a little bit less food or spending less time on our phones? What is the value of giving our stuff to other people? Is Jesus making any sense? Would we be more likely to know God if we practiced these things? Can you believe Lent is all about growing closer to God's love? How?

Repent and Believe

The First Sunday of Lent
Luke 4:1-13

Background information:
- After being baptized (Lk 3:21-22), Jesus is empowered to defeat Satan's temptations.
- "Forty days and nights" that Jesus spent in the desert are an allusion to the forty years Israelites spent in the desert after they had escaped Egypt. Although Israel was unfaithful and turned against God (remember the Golden Calf debacle?), Jesus remains faithful to God despite Satan's best efforts.

Summary: Filled with the Holy Spirit, Jesus is led into the desert to fast, pray, and be close to God. During this time the devil came to tempt him first with food, then with worldly power, and finally with Godly glory. Jesus endures.

Help students reflect: What does it mean to be tempted? How do we know when something is not good for us? How do we handle wanting to do the wrong things while at the same time wanting to do the right thing? What are the most common temptations you face? Why do we need to avoid those things? What can we do? Why would it matter that Jesus was baptized before He dealt with these temptations of Satan? How does baptism help? What does baptism give us? What does it feel like to be filled with the Holy Spirit?

Your Father Who Sees You

Matthew 6:1-6, 16-18

SPRING: TIME — GROWTH

QUADRAGINTA: "40 DAYS" — LENTE: "SPRING"

sketch it
Add to each image to show what the hypocrites do for each of the three.

hypocrites?

fasting   prayer   almsGIVING

explain it
What "reward" have they received?

the acknowledgement or glory of the public, the credit for it.

I'll be fasting on Fridays aside from one meal. I'll be giving up soda for Lent too. I'll skip meats on Fridays of course.

I'll add an extra 20 minutes of personal prayer each day, usually to do rosary. I'm also reading a prayer book.

I'm planning on setting aside all the earnings from my job at the ice cream shop for the season of Lent. I'm giving half of it to Catholic Charities and the other half to the outreach center.

write it
What is your plan for this Lent for each: fasting, prayer, and almsgiving?

explain it
What "repayment" will you receive?

the Kingdom of HEAVEN!

color & reflect
As you color the page, pray about your plans for this Lent. Ask God for guidance and for the willpower and dedication to stick to it and grow in faith this Lent. Don't forget, and don't give up!

Teacher Notes: Gospel Doodle Reflections Cycle Year "C"

LENT

The Transfiguration

The Second Sunday of Lent
Luke 9:28-36

Background information:
- "The mountain" is where Jesus goes to pray.
- Moses and Elijah represent the Old Testament. But, now, Jesus is the one to whom we need to listen.[9]
- The "Exodus" Jesus will accomplish is the leading of humanity from the slavery of sin into the freedom of the Sons of God.[10]

Summary: Jesus takes His closest disciples up the mountain with Him to pray. There, Jesus's appearance is transformed, Moses and Elijah appear with Him, and the three converse. The disciples wake up and want to join the conversation. At that moment, the glory-cloud of God covers the mountain, and the voice of God speaks. The disciples are terrified and do not speak about this moment again until after the resurrection.

Help students reflect: What do you imagine Jesus, Moses, and Elijah spoke about? Why are mountains a good place to pray? Do you think that you could have an experience in life like the one the disciples had? Can you experience through your own prayer and meditation what they experienced on the mountain? Do you think God wants to transfigure your life? What does this mean?

Repentance and Bearing Fruit

The Third Sunday of Lent
Luke 13:1-9

Background information:
- Pilate was a violent man. Ancient history records further acts of violence than presented here in Luke.
- There is a great deal of common sense in the Gospel: not everything bad that happens is caused by sin, but sin does always lead to evil in our lives.
- The Fig Tree parable is a perfect story for Lent: now is the time to try to bear fruit in the next year.

Summary: Jesus first calls the people to repentance, reminding them not to be superstitious, but to take seriously the damage sin does to their lives. Then, in the Parable of the Fig Tree, Jesus reminds us that now is the time to prepare ourselves to bear fruit.

Help students reflect: What kinds of superstitions are believed today? What's the difference between superstition and faith in Jesus? Why does Jesus think that sin is deadly? What would you do if you had a tree that didn't bear any fruit for three years? Would you be as merciful as Jesus? How do we "cultivate the ground" and "fertilize" our lives so that we can live fruitfully?

Teacher Notes: Gospel Doodle Reflections   **Cycle Year "C"**

The Prodigal Son

LENT

The Fourth Sunday of Lent
Luke 15:1-3, 11-32

Background information:
- The younger son asks for the inheritance that would properly have been his at the time of his father's death.
- Swine is not kosher, so the young man has even abandoned his Jewish religion.

Summary: A son, fully rejecting his father, takes his inheritance and leaves town. In his new life the son squanders his wealth until none is left. Then, a famine strikes, and he is starving and forced to take a job tending pigs. He runs home hoping at least to be a servant in his father's house and is surprised to receive a king's welcome. The older son sees the party and is furious that his brother, who committed such evil, was treated so mercifully. The story ends with the father hoping to explain his mercy to the embittered son.

Help students reflect: Which character in the story do you connect with most, and why? Do any of the characters act rationally? What was wrong about what the younger son did? How bad was it really, what the younger son did? Say it in your own words. How could the father be so merciful? What would it have felt like for the father to see his son coming home at a distance? Can we imagine that God treats us that way? Are our priests like this? Does this story remind us of the Sacrament of Confession? Why or why not?

The Woman Caught in Adultery

The Fifth Sunday of Lent
John 8:1-11

Background information:
- Much has been made of Jesus's writing in the ground. There may be a connection to Jeremiah 17:13. There are as many theories as scholars.[11]
- There is a definite connection to Deuteronomy 17:7 which prescribes death as the penalty as well as witnesses to throw the first stones.[12]

Summary: Jesus teaches a crowd when Pharisees come to tempt Jesus. They present a woman caught in adultery. Their goal is to force Jesus to have to choose between either being cruel or contradicting the Mosaic Law. Jesus reminds the Pharisees of their own sinfulness. Jesus tells the woman he does not condemn her and sends her away with the penance to sin no more.

Help students reflect: Why do the Pharisees try to test Jesus? What were they trying to prove? What do the Pharisees mean by "law"? How does Jesus treat the Mosaic Law? How are Christians called to treat civil laws? Why does no one condemn the woman? Why does Jesus not condemn her and why does he tell her to sin no more? What is Jesus trying to teach us about God? What about how we treat others? How does this story relate to the season of Lent?

Teacher Notes: Gospel Doodle Reflections Cycle Year "C"

LENT

The Passion of the Lord

Palm Sunday
Luke 22:14-23:56

Background information:
- The Passover Feast is a Jewish celebration of their release from slavery in Egypt and flight through the Red Sea and into the desert. The feast begins after the Passover Lamb is sacrificed in the temple at sundown. Jesus changes the ritual to insert Himself as the Passover Lamb that will be sacrificed on the cross so that we all might be freed from slavery to sin and begin our journey to our own Promised Land.[13]
- It is interesting that Jesus knew Judas would betray Him. Why keep Judas around? Why invite Judas to celebrate the Passover? Why would Jesus make that decision?

Summary: In His final moments, Jesus shows his friends true love and gives them the tools to understand why He gave Himself up to suffering and death. By reinventing a Jewish ritual of salvation, by keeping a betrayer in the ranks of His friends, and by turning His cheek to the unjust beatings of sinful men all the way to His own death, Jesus gives us the ultimate lesson in human patience, love, friendship, mercy, forgiveness, understanding, and goodness. Everything it is to be a person, Jesus puts on display for us, out of love for us in the final act of His life.

Help students reflect: Which part of the passion story means the most to you? What part is most impactful? Why did Jesus have a Last Supper with all His disciples? Why did He leave us the Eucharist? What does it mean that someone **died** for you?

The Last Supper

Holy Thursday
John 13:1-15

Background information:
- The work of washing another's feet was relegated to a slave, which explains why Peter was so shocked by Jesus's action.[14]
- The foot washing is a symbol of Jesus's whole humiliating passion, but also of the Eucharist itself. Jesus humbles Himself so that we can receive Him, and so that we can do likewise to those around us. The foot washing is a Christian call to action as is the Eucharist we celebrate every Sunday.

Summary: At their last meal together, Jesus washes the feet of the disciples. John lets us know that Judas had already decided to betray Jesus at this point. The disciples protest the foot washing, but Jesus tells them unequivocally, if they don't let him serve them, they will not receive His inheritance.

Help students reflect: It seems weird to us that Jesus would wash another man's feet. But 2,000 years ago in Jerusalem there was a lot of sand and dust. Feet got dirty. Slaves were employed to wash feet. Now Jesus takes on this role for us. He serves us as a slave. Can Jesus still be God if He humbles Himself this much for us? Did you know that the Eucharist was connected to this action? What does that mean for your reception of the Eucharist? Did Jesus wash Judas's feet?

The Passion of the Lord

draw it

Draw a gift box or gift bag around the Eucharist and decorate it while you pray a prayer of thanks to Jesus for the gift of His most precious body and blood.

explain it

What does Passover remember as a Jewish celebration?
It celebrates their freedom from slavery in Egypt.
— Begin journey to "Promised Land"

What is the significance of the Passover Lamb in relation to Jesus's sacrifice?
He becomes the lamb now — sacrificed to free us!
— Begin journey to Heaven!

Use sketches or words with creative lettering to show what Jesus is revealing about the future with each of these statements:

1. "I have eagerly desired to eat this Passover with you before I suffer."

2. "From this time on I shall not drink of the fruit of the vine until the kingdom of God comes."

3. "This is my body, which will be given for you."

4. "The hand of the one who is to betray me is with me on the table."

5. "I tell you, Peter, before the cock crows this day, you will deny three times that you know me."

Luke 22:14-23:56

Sketch it

Teacher Notes: Gospel Doodle Reflections　　　　　　　　　　**Cycle Year "C"**

The Death of Jesus Christ

Good Friday
John 18:1-19:42

Background information:
- Peter was Jesus's best friend when he denied that he even knew Jesus.
- Crucifixion was public murder: a state-sponsored terrorism reserved for men and women who acted against the Roman Empire.
- Philosophers and theologians have interpreted Jesus's line, "It is finished," not only as the end of Jesus's life but as the "finishing" or "completion" of human history.

Summary: Jesus is betrayed by Judas and taken away by the Jewish temple guards. Jesus is tried by the Jewish authorities in a mock trial and convicted while He is abandoned by most of His disciples. The Jews take Jesus to Pilate, the local Roman governor, because only Romans had authority to crucify. Pilate finds Jesus innocent, but obeys the pressure of the mob, has Jesus scourged, and hands Jesus over for crucifixion. Jesus dies nailed to a cross and is buried.

Help students reflect: Do we know anyone in our lives who is treated unfairly? Are there members of our own families who are unjustly accused? Are our friends bullied and mocked? Do we ourselves sometimes receive bad treatment we don't deserve?

Why didn't Jesus run away? The garden exists on the edge of Jerusalem: Jesus could have disappeared into the night. Why did He stay?

What do Jesus's last moments of life teach us about bullying and the way God responds to those who have been treated unjustly?

LENT

Teacher Notes: Gospel Doodle Reflections **Cycle Year "C"**

The Empty Tomb

Easter Sunday
John 20:1-9

Background information:
- The crucifixion and the empty tomb are two of the best documented events in human history.
- The resurrection is the most influential event in documented human history.
- The tomb was guarded by Roman soldiers, but John found it empty. The arrangement of the burial cloths in the tomb made John believe that it had not been robbed, and that Jesus had risen from the dead as He had promised.

Summary: On Sunday, Mary of Magdala (and perhaps some other women) went to the tomb in grief, but Mary was stunned to find the tomb open and empty. She ran to the disciples and found Simon Peter and John, who then ran to see for themselves what had happened. The disciples found the tomb empty and slowly began to believe that Jesus had risen.

Help students reflect: What does it mean to you that life conquered death, light conquers darkness, hope conquers despair, faith conquers disbelief?
What are some obstacles that people have to belief in the Resurrection? God is powerful enough to deal with those obstacles, but do you believe it?
Where in your own life do you need to see a little resurrection?

Divine Mercy Sunday
John 20:19-31

Background information:
- Don't forget these are the same disciples who betrayed Jesus a little bit before His appearance to them.
- Resurrected Jesus still appears in human form but is able to enter into locked rooms.
- The breathing calls to mind the breath of life God breathed into Adam in Genesis. Now Jesus gives new life to the disciples who had been "dead" because of grief and despair. [15]

Summary: After Jesus's death by mob violence, His disciples had to hide themselves from the rest of the Jewish community which was seeking to root out any remnants of Jesus. In a locked room, they gathered in secret for several days, until finally Jesus appeared to them in person, at once. Jesus gave them peace and showed them His scars. The disciples were able to rejoice again and received the Holy Spirit. Together with the Holy Spirit, Jesus gave them the authority to forgive sins.

Help students reflect: Would it be easier to believe in God and God's promises if your life was more peaceful? What makes life stressful? What separates you from the peace God wants to give you? Some common answers are: too much technology, fighting with siblings, lying, etc. Jesus gave the disciples authority to forgive sins. Today that authority remains with our bishops and is passed to us through our priests. What does confession mean to you?

Teacher Notes: Gospel Doodle Reflections   **Cycle Year "C"**

Follow Me

Third Sunday of Easter
John 21:1-19

Background information:
- This Gospel is composed of two post-Resurrection stories of Jesus. One, a meal with a whole group of disciples and another, an intimate encounter between Jesus and Peter.
- The sons of Zebedee are James and John, also called the "sons of thunder."
- After the death of Jesus, Peter has returned to his old fishing profession. He has given up on the mission Jesus gave the disciples and is returning to his old way of life.
- In the discourse between Jesus and John, two different Greek verbs for "love" are used. Jesus asks, "do you love me?" Peter basically responds, "I like you." This is enough for Jesus to work with.

Summary: After the crucifixion, the disciples return to their old ways of life. While fishing, Jesus appears, helps them attain a huge catch, and they all share breakfast. Then, Jesus takes Peter aside and charges him to tend the sheep. Peter reveals his weak love, but Jesus accepts it.

Help students reflect: When we listen to Jesus, things work out better than we can imagine. Does anyone in your family have a story like this? What does it mean to you that Jesus shares meals with us? Does this remind us of Mass? Jesus says, "Follow me." Where is Jesus leading you in life? Where is Jesus asking you to follow him? Trust Him and He will not lead you astray!

The Father and I Are One

Fourth Sunday of Easter
John 10:27-30

Background information:
- Shepherding and sheep were ubiquitous in ancient culture. They were part of daily life, like delivery trucks or fast food. So, when Jesus says, "My sheep hear my voice . . ., they follow me," that is exactly how everyone in Jesus's audience knew sheep to behave towards their shepherds and they understood that Jesus was like a shepherd to His disciples.
- Even today, shepherds can still recognize more than one thousand of their own sheep just by looking at their face!

Summary: This Gospel is a theological statement that can be summed up in two statements: 1) Jesus is God, 2) Jesus saves His people.

Help students reflect: What does the sheep analogy make you think of? Has anyone ever spent any time with sheep before? What does it mean to you today that Jesus, a person, is also God? Is that strange? Why might that be a good thing? What does it mean that Jesus and the Father are one? Aren't they two? What can you make of this mystery? Do you know what the church teaches about this? (Look at Catechism paragraphs 232-260).

Teacher Notes: Gospel Doodle Reflections

Cycle Year "C"

EASTER

Love One Another

Fifth Sunday of Easter
John 13:31-33a, 34-35

Background information:
- There's a little piece of verse 33 missing in the Gospel reading. That's because the rest of the text, which sounds exclusionary, would be difficult for most people to understand from the pulpit.
- Jesus takes the commandment "love one another" from Leviticus 19:18. But what is "new" here is that Jesus can give commandments like God, because He is God.[16]

Summary: This speech of Jesus's is taken from His long homily on the night of the Last Supper (John chapters 13-17). This section falls after Jesus announces Judas's betrayal and before Jesus predicts Peter's denial. This literary perspective shows us that the glory of God is in the fact that Jesus loves us no matter what—even when His best friends betray and deny Him—and that God is glorified when Jesus's disciples love others in the same way.

Help students reflect: Why did Jesus love Judas and Peter so much even when one betrayed Him and the other denied Him? Does that give us confidence that Jesus loves us even when we sin or forget about Him? I hope so! Do people recognize us as disciples of Jesus? That would be a good goal for this week or for the whole year! Be recognized not just for wearing Jesus-themed T-shirts, but for loving others.

Wordsearch answers:

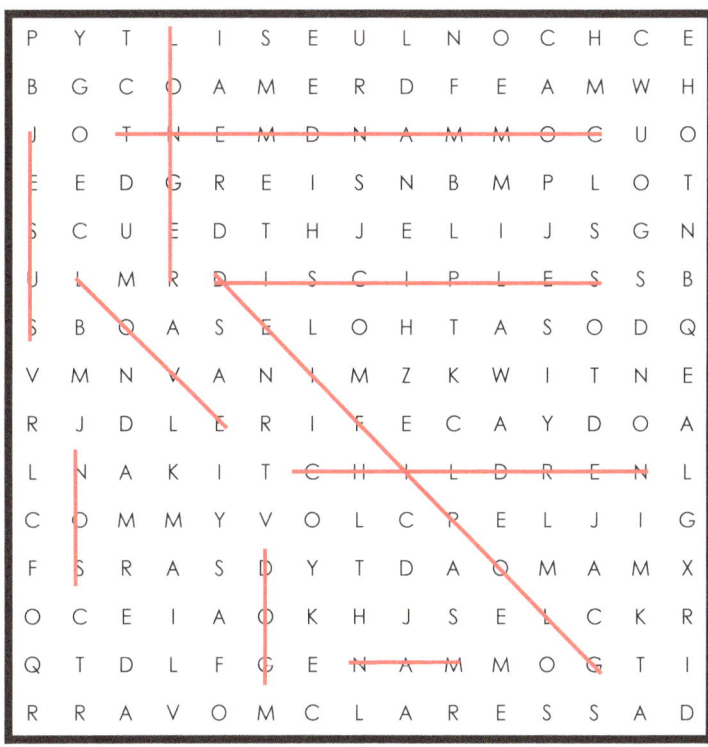

Teacher Notes: Gospel Doodle Reflections Cycle Year "C"

EASTER

Do Not Let Your Hearts Be Troubled

Sixth Sunday of Easter
John 14:23-29

Background information:
- This Gospel continues our journey through Jesus's Last Supper homily.
- The Trinity is a major theme here. Jesus tells us the Holy Spirit is The Advocate and that the Holy Spirit is sent by the Father and will teach us everything and remind us of Jesus. Then, later, Jesus says that the Father is greater than Jesus is because Jesus was sent by the Father. Although all three are equally God, we can understand the Father is first in order.
- Here again, is a good opportunity to be reminded what the church teaches about the Trinity. Look at Catechism paragraphs 232-260.

Summary: Jesus continues a number of themes during this part of His Last Supper homily: (1) the connection between love and keeping Jesus's word, (2) that Jesus's words are from the Father, (3) the Father sent Jesus and the Holy Spirit, (4) Jesus gives us peace, and (5) Jesus predicts His return to the Father (the Ascension).

Help students reflect: Meditate on this passage from the Catechism: "The goal of the whole divine household is the entry of God's creatures [read 'us'] into the perfect unity of the Blessed Trinity" (p.260). We are destined for perfect love, forever, with the Trinity. How does that make you feel? What do you think that will be like? What will it look like? When Jesus says, "do not let your hearts be troubled or afraid," what does that make you think of?

Teacher Notes: Gospel Doodle Reflections   **Cycle Year "C"**

EASTER

Seventh Sunday of Easter
John 17:20-26

Background information:
- Jesus finishes His Last Supper homily by speaking about unity and love among God and Jesus's disciples. In John's Gospel, these are the last verses prior to Jesus's arrest in Chapter 18.
- The whole Last Supper homily is one long prayer of Jesus (addressed to the Father).
- John's Gospel, of the four, is the one most influenced by Greek philosophy, which saw unity and oneness as the perfection of the world.
- John's Gospel contains the greatest poetry of the four gospels.

Summary: At the conclusion of His Last Supper homily, Jesus prays again to the Father for unity among His disciples and between His disciples and God. He prays and teaches that this unity will be their glory, their perfection, and the cause of love in the world. Finally, He restates His mission: sent by the Father, to make the Father known, that the love of the Father may be in the world.

Help students reflect: Where in the world do we need to see more unity and oneness? Are unity and oneness possible in families or churches? What about between religious groups?
If there was more oneness and unity between Christians, would people see more of the love of the Father in the world? Who is one person we can pray to be more united with in our own lives?

Ascension of Our Lord
Luke 24:46-53

Background information:
- The Ascension is meant to show something of the destiny of a Christian. We will die, be resurrected by the power of God, and be brought to live together with Jesus and the Father in some way. The details of that journey are still a mystery.
- The disciples returned to the Jewish temple in Jerusalem to praise Jesus, because they were still practicing Jews at that time. In fact, it would not be until about forty years after the death of Jesus that the Christians would be thrown out of the Jewish synagogues and condemned for their belief in Jesus.

Summary: Jesus catechizes the disciples for a last time, promises them the Holy spirit (the promise of my Father), blesses them, and disappears from their sight.

Help students reflect: What do you hope Heaven will be like? What do you know about the way other religions talk about Heaven, Paradise, or the Afterlife? Is there anything unique about the Christian way of looking at things? What does "the promise of the Father" mean to you? Why is the Holy Spirit the promise of the Father? What does that do for us? What kind of gift or promise is this? Are you witnesses of these things: Christ's passion, death, and resurrection, repentance and the forgiveness of sins, or the preaching of the Gospel?

Teacher Notes: Gospel Doodle Reflections — Cycle Year "C"

Peace Be With You

Pentecost
John 20:19-23

Background information:
- Just as God 'breathed' life into Adam (Genesis) so now Jesus breathes new life into His disciples.
- This also recalls for us Ezekiel 37 and the "dry bones."[17]
- The Gifts of the Holy Spirit are seven: wisdom, understanding, counsel, fortitude, knowledge, piety, and fear of the Lord. The Fruits of the Holy Spirit are twelve: charity, joy, peace, patience, kindness, goodness, generosity, gentleness, faithfulness, modesty, self-control, and chastity.

Summary: While the disciples were hiding from the Jewish authorities after the crucifixion, Jesus appears to them that they might believe in the Resurrection. Jesus gives them His peace, shows them the wounds in His hands and side and then sends them on a mission to forgive sins.

Help students reflect: Jesus wanted to give His disciples three things after He rose from the dead:
1. Tangible proof that He's real.
2. Peace in the depths of their hearts.
3. The authority to give peace to others.

What would proof that He is real look like to you? Where/when have you felt completely at peace before? Has anyone ever helped you to overcome your restlessness, being stressed out, or being ashamed? What was that like? Do you believe that Jesus wants to come to give these things to you?

EASTER

Teacher Notes: Gospel Doodle Reflections   **Cycle Year "C"**

Immaculate Conception

Feast of the Immaculate Conception of Mary
Luke 1:26-38

Background information: Some people mistakenly think that the Immaculate Conception is about Jesus being conceived, but it is actually about Mary being conceived without sin from the very beginning of her life.

Summary: Mary is "full of grace" to the point that she is completely without sin. She is pure and free of the stain and corruption that other humans are susceptible to because of original sin. Her special sanctifying grace was present from before her own birth, as she was blessed by God in advance. She would bear Jesus, and therefore God's grace made her holy and pure.

Help students reflect: What does this show about God's plan for Jesus, that He made Mary immaculate from her conception and through her entire life? How can I strive to be more like Mary, despite my own imperfection? How would I answer such a large request or challenge from God if an angel came to me? How would my own response compare to Mary's reply of "may it be done to me according to your word."?

Mary, Mother of God

Solemnity of Mary, Holy Mother of God
Luke 2:16-21

Background information: Mary had followed through with God's plan, and we celebrate her as the Mother of God. We have many titles for Mary because she is so special.

Summary: Jesus is finally born, a God coming to earth through human birth, made possible through Mary. This incredible event did not go unnoticed by the shepherds, and would later come to be known throughout the entire world. Mary is the human mother to a newborn baby who is both God and man. As the Mother of God, we honor her.

Help students reflect: Mary "kept all these things, reflecting on them in her heart." Put yourself in Mary's position for a moment in your imagination. How do you think it felt for the shepherds to come visit her newborn, after knowing what the angel had told her. Now think ahead to Jesus's adult life. We know His future, and the suffering Mary would have to endure later on in His story. She was central to something incredibly special, that caused the shepherds to glorify God. Jesus was such a gift! Think about Mary's part in all of this and what her reflections in her heart may have been.

HOLY DAYS

Teacher Notes: Gospel Doodle Reflections — Cycle Year "C"

HOLY DAYS

Feast of the Assumption
Luke 1:39-56

Background information:
- Sometimes, Mary is compared to the Ark of the Covenant, because she carried / held God's word (come to life!)
- Pope Pius XII declared Mary's Assumption into Heaven as part of our official "dogma" for Catholics in 1950.
- There is a difference between the word used for Jesus **ascending** into heaven, and Mary being **assumed** into heaven, because Jesus rose up out of his own power while Mary was assumed out of God's power, not her own.

Summary: This feast day is about Mary being assumed into heaven, body and soul. She was without sin and was pure. To honor her, God carried her right up to heaven without her having to die in the same way that we do. She is now considered "Queen of Heaven."

Help students reflect: Think how challenging Mary's life on earth was. She had to watch her son suffer and die in a horrible way. Can you see why Jesus saved her from having to go through the same bodily death that we all must endure? What an honor, to be the only human to ever enter the kingdom of Heaven without her body having to go through the usual earthly decay. Her body was sacred to God and she is still very much respected by all of us today.

All Saints Day
Matthew 5:1-12a

Background information:
- Saints (with a capital "S") are canonized, official saints. When we use a lowercase "s" for the word saints, it represents all of the people in heaven. All of the good people of God who have died and gone to heaven are part of the communion of saints.
- All Souls Day is different from All Saints Day because it also includes the faithful people who have died that are not yet in heaven (like those in purgatory). They may be repentant, but have not yet fully entered into the glory of heaven.
- This holy day was originally started to honor martyrs (those who died for their faith).

Summary: This feast day is for celebrating all of the saints, both known and unknown. They are often also referred to as the "faithful departed," because they have died and are in the kingdom of heaven.

Help students reflect: This is a good day to learn about a Saint or choose a favorite Saint. You might be surprised how much you have in common with some of the canonized Saints if you do a little research. Say a prayer that you will someday become a saint in heaven yourself.

All Saints Day

You may be hoping to join the communion of saints someday, but have you prepared or are you ***just*** hoping? Just like you'd need to prepare for an amazing vacation, you need to prepare for an eternal life in advance if you want to go. Pack up everything you will need by listing the items you know you will need to get to your destination. Use creative lettering and sketches to include the proper items in each bag. You'll need to prepare by gathering up a wardrobe full of love for others, load up plenty of relationship building with God, and even prepare your own heart and soul. Pack up for the rest our your journey on this earth, and for the adventure awaiting you in God's kingdom!

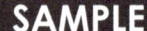

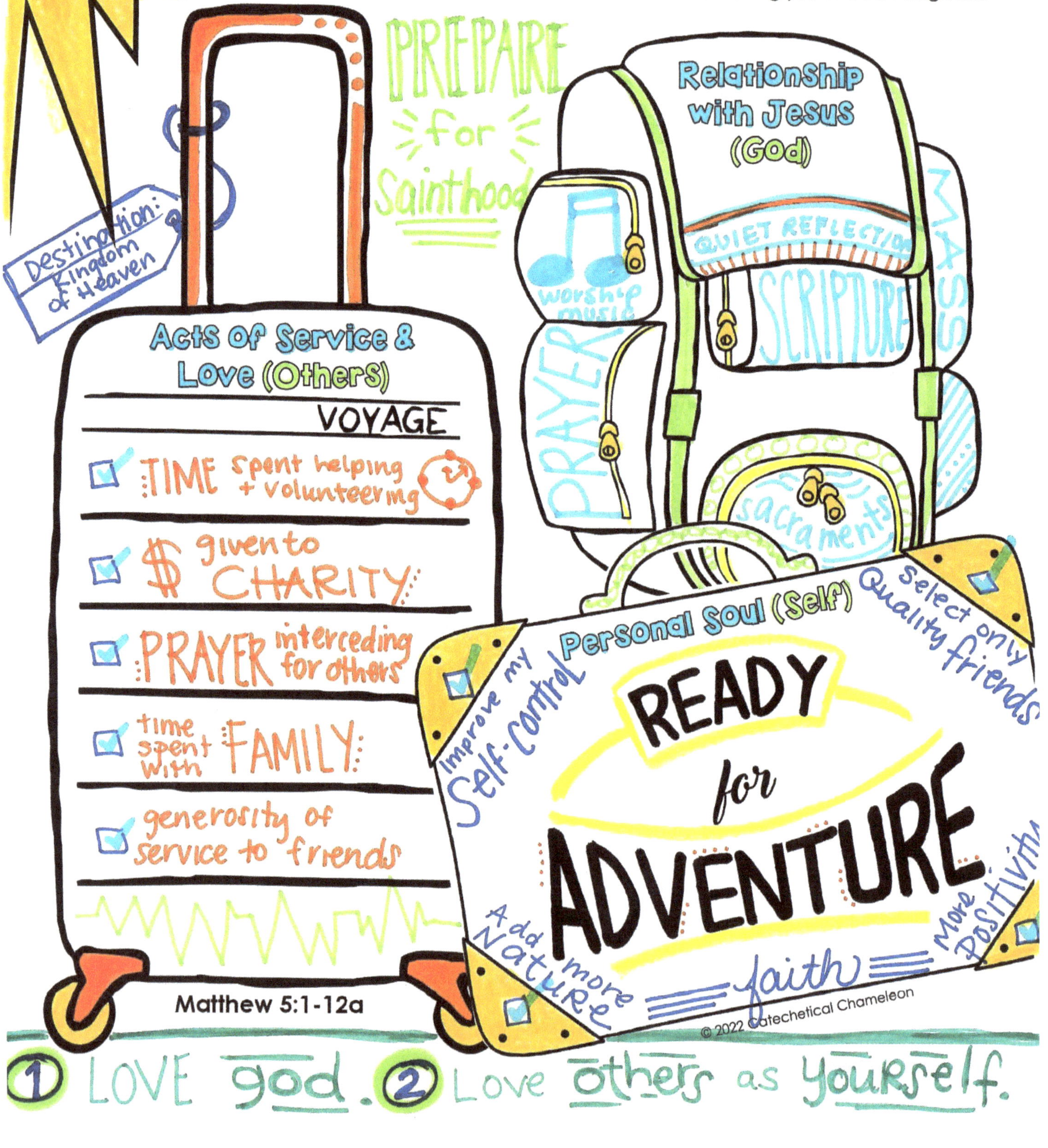

BONUS PAGES

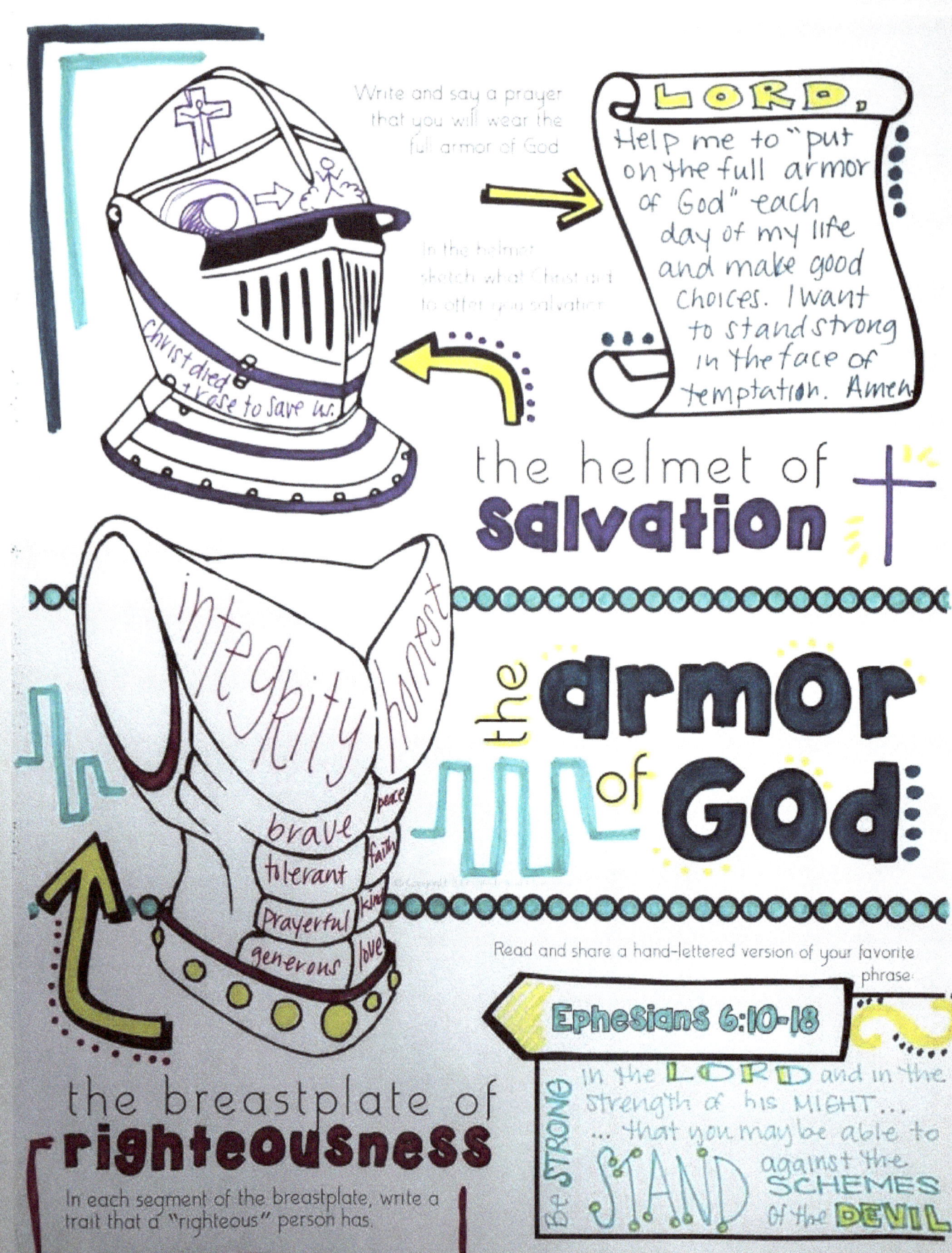

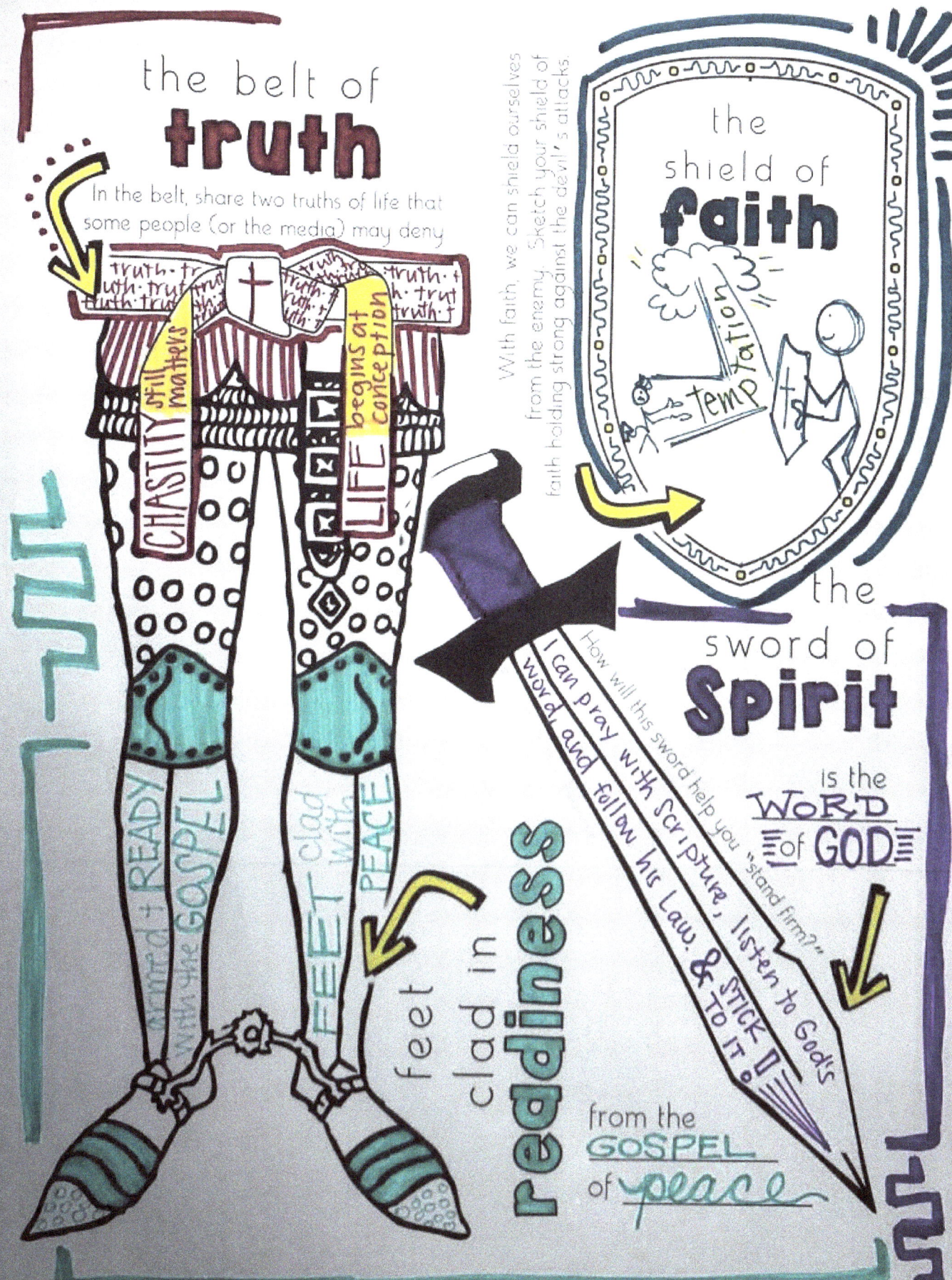

- ☐ Color the words around the perimeter of the calendar using the color listed.
- ☐ Fill in the blanks to show what each color represents.
- ☐ Write the season of the church year inside each sector.
- ☐ Show the seasons of the regular calendar year outside of the circle.

Name: Answer Key / Teacher Guide

The Liturgical Calendar

© copyright 2016 Catechetical Chameleon

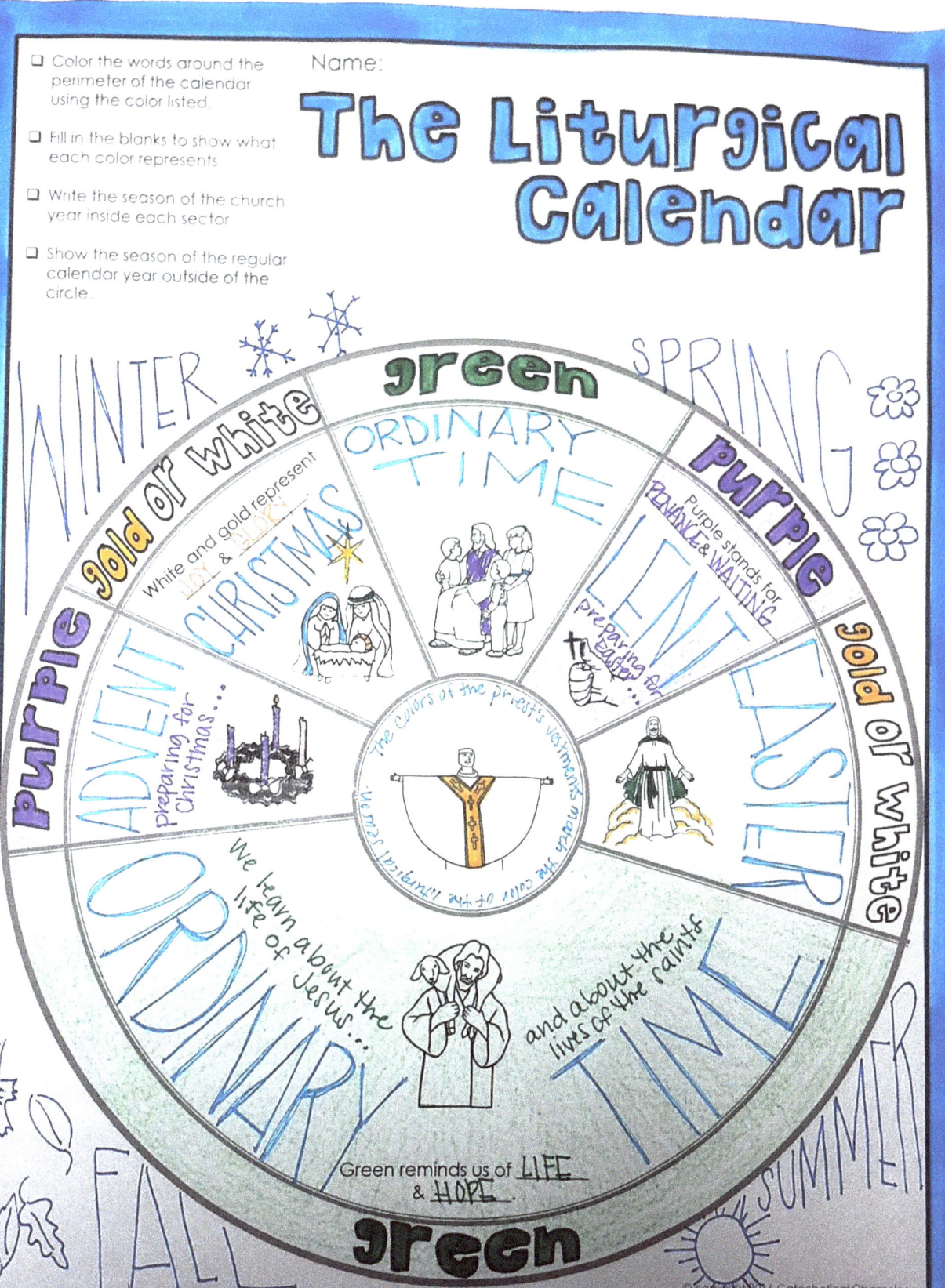

doodle notebook

footnotes

Cycle Year "C"

All citations are taken from the text and footnotes of the NABRE:

"The New American Bible Revised Edition ©2010." In The Catholic Study Bible: Second Edition. Edited by Donald Senior, John J. Collins, and Mary Ann Getty. New York: Oxford University Press, 2011. Nihil Obstat: Stephen J. Hartdegen, O.F.M., S.S.L, Censor Deputatis. Imprimatur: †James A. Hickey, J.C.D., Archbishop of Washington, August 27th, 1986.

1 "New American Bible Revised Edition," footnote for Luke 21:26, in The Catholic Study Bible: Second Edition (New York: Oxford Publishing, 2011): page 1478.

2 Ibid., footnote for Luke 3:16, pg. 1442.

3 Ibid., footnote for Luke 2:41-52, pg. 1440.

4 Ibid., footnote for Matthew 2:1, pg. 1338.

5 Ibid., footnote for Matthew 2:11, pg. 1338.

6 Ibid., footnote for Luke 3:19-20, pg. 1442.

7 Ibid., footnote for Luke 6:20-26, pg. 1448.

8 Ibid., footnote for Luke 16:1-8a, pg. 1468.

9 Ibid., footnote for Luke 9:30, pg. 1455.

10 Ibid., footnote for Luke 9:31, pg. 1456.

11 Ibid., footnote for John 8:6, pg. 1503.

12 Ibid., footnote for John 8:5, pg. 1503.

13 Ibid., footnote for Luke 22:15, pg. 1479.

14 Ibid., footnote for John 13:5, pg. 1512.

15 Ibid., footnote for John 20:22, pg. 1524.

16 Ibid., footnote for John 13:34, pg. 1513.

17 Ibid., footnote for John 20:22, pg. 1524.

www.ingramcontent.com/pod-product-compliance
Lightning Source LLC
Chambersburg PA
CBHW042358070526
44585CB00029B/2979